Com
& An
Dictionary

D1028177

Edited by Garth Gardner, Ph.D.

G G
c
®

11/03

GARTH GARDNER COMPANY

GGC publishing

Washington DC, USA · London, UK

Team: Ali Lam, Gayle Green, Chris Gosnell, Amiee Beck,
Ryan Bell, Malek Z. Abdo.
Art Director: Nic Banks
Illustrator: Tomoko Miki
Cover Designer: Tomoko Miki

Editorial inquiries concerning this book should be e-mailed to:
info@ggcinc.com. Website: www.gogardner.com

Library of Congress Cataloging-in-Publication Data

Printed in Canada

Gardner's computer graphics & animation dictionary.
     p. cm.
Includes bibliographical references.
  ISBN 1-58965-005-0 (paper back)
  1. Animation (Cinematography)—Dictionaries. 2. Computer
animation—Dictionaries. 3. Computer graphics—Dictionaries. I.
Garth
Gardner Company.
TR897.5 .G37 2002
778.5'347—dc21

                    2002152071

About this Book

Gardner's CG & Animation Dictionary is the consummate guide to the language of the computer graphics and animation world. It contains short and quick definitions of production terms used by visual effects and animation professionals. Hundreds of terms and phrases are defined as well as acronyms and terms related to software packages. Ideal for students and working professionals, this reference is packed with technical, non-technical, career-related titles, and production language. Cel Animation, Clay Animation, Anime, CGI, and all other styles and techniques of animation are also defined along with common graphic design terms. This guide will keep novices and professionals up-to-date in this fast-moving world of Graphics & Animation.

About the Author

Garth Gardner, Ph.D. is a fine artist and animation producer. He has taught and lectured at several universities including The Ohio State University, William Paterson University, University of California Los Angeles, Fashion Institute of Technology, Florida A&M University, University of Southern California, University of Texas at Austin, Xavier University, and George Mason University. He is a graduate of San Francisco State University and The Ohio State University.

Numbers

1-Bit Color: The number of copies per pixel that a graphics file can store. Each pixel is represented by one bit, which only has one of two states or colors. 1-bit pixels are either black or white.

8-Bit Color/Grayscale: Each pixel is represented by eight bits, which can have 256 colors or shades of gray (as in a grayscale image).

12-Field: Refers to a standard cel size of approximately 12.5"x10.5".

16-Bit Color: Can display up to 65,356 colors.

16-Field: This term refers to a standard cel size of approximately 15.5" wide by 12.5" tall.

16:9 Aspect Ratio: The standard display aspect ratio of DVD-Video. When displayed on television screen (which is 4:3), 16:9 materials will be "letterboxed" with black bars at top and bottom of screen.

24-Bit Color: Provides 16.7 million colors per pixel. Bits are divided into three bytes: one for each red, green, and blue components of a pixel and can be photographic in quality. Also known as True Color on Microsoft Windows and Millions of Color on Macs.

2D: Two-dimensional.

2D Graphics: Two-dimensional graphics. Images that utilize only two spatial coordinates, height and width (x, y).

3:2 Pulldown: The ratio between film and video frames that occurs as a result of the telecine transfer when film's

---

24fps (frames per second) have to be stretched to fill video's 30fps.

3D: Three-dimensional.

3D Audio: A technique used to give more depth to traditional stereo sound. Typically, placing a device in a room with stereo speakers produces 3D audio. This device dynamically analyzes speaker sound and sends feedback to the sound system for readjustment to give the impression that the speakers are further apart. Popular when improving computer audio, when speakers tend to be small and close. There are several that attach to computer sound cards. Also known as 3D Sound.

3D Computer Animator: The process of creating models within computer memory, applying textures, setting up the choreography, or movement, of the 3D objects, lights, or cameras.

3D Computer Modeler: See 3D Modeling.

3D Graphics: The process of creating models within computer memory, setting up lights, and applying textures. When a computer is instructed from which angle to view the 3D scene, it will generate an image simulating the defined conditions.

3D Modeling: The process of creating representations of objects and spaces with the goal of viewing them from all three visible dimensions.

3D Pipeline: Three-dimensional graphics can be divided into three stages: tessellation, which creates a described model of an object, which is then converted to a set of polygons. This term also describes geometry, which includes transformation, lighting, setup, and rendering, which is critical for 3D image quality. It creates a 2D display from the polygons created in the geometry stage.

4:1:1 Color: Moderately compressed video color subsampling in which the luminance channel is not subsampled but the chrominance channel has one-quarter resolution. Most DV formats, including miniDV, use 4:1:1 color.

4:2:0 Color: Moderately compressed video color subsampling very similar to 4:1:1; the standard MPEG color.

4:2:2 Color: Mildly compressed video color subsampling in which the luminance channel is not subsampled but the chrominance channel has resolution. Commonly used in professional video formats, such as BetaCamSP.

4:3 Aspect Ratio: A common display aspect ratio. For example, 320 x 240 is a 4:3 aspect frame size.

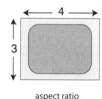

aspect ratio

4:4:4 Color: Uncompressed video color which has no subsampling.

45-Degree Angle Spotlight Pair: A simple, effective way to create generous amounts of light revealing subject features as well as some shadow detail.

56K Line: A data transmission line capable of moving information at 56,000bps (bytes per second).

586: The unofficial name of the Intel Pentium processor, named for its marketability and for its easily protected copyright laws. Many within the computer industry referred to the Pentium processor as the 586 in reference to its predecessors, the 286, 386, and 486. It's also the name given to Pentium-class processors produced by Intel Corporation competitors.

686: The name given to Pentium Pro-class processors produced by Intel Corporation competitors.

6DOF (Six Degrees Of Freedom): Yaw, pitch, roll, up/down, left/right, front/back (or pan, zoom, swivel).

A

ACM: Association of Computing Machinery. The organization responsible for hosting SIGGRAPH.

Active Server: An end system with a specific general purpose OS. It is also an active node that offers more user flexibility that can be considered as an end system with a full protocol stack. It provides an execution environment capable of running user-provided processes that are unrestricted above the transport layer.

Active Server Pages: See ASP.

Active Steaming Format: See ASF.

Actors: Representations of players performing actions for them, as in the Mandala system. See also Agent, Character, and CAD.

Actualizing: Existing.

AD: See Assistant Director.

Adaptive Differential Pulse Code Modulation (ADPCM): A compression technique which encodes the difference between one sample and the next. Variations are lossy and lossless.

Adaptive Interaction: A type of interactivity in which the content of a program is adapted to meet users' needs based upon users' input.

Adaptive Noise Reduction Filter: An "intelligent" noise-filtering system that analyzes each pixel and applies an appropriate filter to remove the noise. This maintains edge detail while improving compression.

Adaptive Space Subdivision: This term refers to the process of breaking up the scene space into several small regions, only when needed. Often used by ray tracers. For example, Octrees and BSP trees are subdivision algorithms that can be adaptive.

ADC: See Analog to Digital Conversion.

Additional Dialog Recording (ADR): Dubbing done in addition to or as a substitution for location sound. The term ADR has a certain appeal, as it obscures the fact that dubbing was involved when it appears in the credits of the film.

Additive Blending: A texture-blending method that uses the additive color model. Pixels of base and light maps are blended to make brighter texture. See also Additive Color Model, Additive Transparency, Average Blending, Invert Blending, and Subtractive Blending.

Additive Color Mixing: Color models that mix colors to simulate the way light works when different colored lights are mixed. The result is a brighter color as opposed to subtractive color mixing; adjusting gray or color levels in an image; a 2D line graph represents the incoming and outgoing brightness/color values.

Additive Color: In video, the combination of red, green, and blue phosphors to generate all other colors. See also Average Transparency.

Adhesive Binding: A binding technique in which single leaves are held together using an adhesive rather than a sewn attachment. See also Perfect Binding.

Adhesive: A substance capable of holding materials together by surface attachment.

ADI: See Area of Dominant Influence.

ADO (Ampex Digital Optics): The trade name for digital effects system manufactured and sold by Ampex.

Adobe Illustrator: An Adobe Systems, Inc. graphics software product used to produce high-quality, low-maintenance Web pages.

Adobe Photoshop: An Adobe Systems, Inc. image-editing software product used to manipulate and produce images for print or Web pages.

Adobe Premiere: An Adobe Systems, Inc. professional digital video editing software program.

ADPCM: See Adaptive Differential Pulse Code Modulation.

ADR: See Automatic Dialog Replacement.

ADSL: See Asymmetric Digital Subscriber Line.

ADU: See Audience Deficiency Unit.

Advance: On a composite print, the distance between a point on the soundtrack and the corresponding image.

Advanced Audio Coder: See AAC.

Advanced Research Projects Agency (ARPANet): The experimental network, established in the 1970s, where the theories and software on which the Internet is based were tested.

Advanced Television: Television that has a higher resolution than a standard NTSC system.

Advertising: The act of calling public attention to a product, service, or event via print, video, or audio.

Aerial-Image Printer: A modified optical printer or animation stand that capitalizes on the fact that a projected image can be suspended in thin air.

Aesthetics: A branch of philosophy dealing with the nature, creation, and appreciation of beauty.

AFC: See Automatic Frequency Control.

Affine: Any transformation composed from rotations, translations, dilatations, (expansions and contractions), and shears.

AFM: See Audio Frequency Modulation.

AGC: See Automatic Gain Control.

AI: See Artificial Intelligence.

AIFF (Audio Interchange File Format): A format developed by Apple Computers to store sounds in the data fork of files; can be played by a variety of downloadable software on both PC and Mac. Common file extensions for AIFF files include .aif, .aiff, and .aifc.

AIFF-C: Audio Interchange File Format with Compression.

AIGA: See American Institute of Graphic Arts.

Airbrush: An atomizer used to apply a fine spray with compressed air.

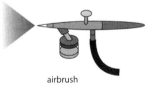

airbrush

Album Cover: A protective cover used with sound recordings; may include important information about performances, or illustrative material.

Album: A book with blank pages used for assembling and presenting a collection. See also Scrapbook.

ALC: See Automatic Level Control.

Alias: The name given to a popular high-end 3D software company that later merged to form Alias/Wavefront and created a software known as MAYA. See also Aliasing.

Aliasing: A term used in graphic design. Aliasing occurs when a computer monitor, printer, or graphics file does not have a high enough resolution to represent a graphic image or text. An aliased image is often said to have the "jaggies."

Alignment: Text positioning. Text can be positioned to the left, right, or center of a page. For the most consistent alignment, Web graphic designers use tables and embedded tables.

Alkaline Paper: Paper having a buffer or reserve of alkaline substance, usually of 10-20 percent precipitated calcium or magnesium carbonate. See also Acid-Free Paper, Permanent Paper.

Allocentric: The opposite of egocentric. For example, bird's eye view or adopting another person's viewpoint.

Alpha-Alias: The blending of pixel colors on the perimeter of hard-edged shapes to smooth undesirable edges ("jaggies").

Alpha Blending: A technique used to create a transparency and a value added to the pixels of a texture map to define simplicity of seeing through the pixel. Used to look through objects, creating effects such as realistic water and glass. Different levels are available, and blurring is often used to create realistic images.

Alpha Buffer: The collective name given to the alpha values for every pixel of an image or bitmap.

Alpha Channel: An additional piece of information stored for a pixel that represents the pixel's transparency. An image, composed of many pixels, often has separate channels for red, green and blue.

Alpha Mix: A way of combining two images. The alpha channel dictates the way mixing is performed.

Alpha Test: The first round of testing on new media products to correct errors in design, content and functionality.

ALT Attribute: A part of the image source tag in HTML. Text should always be included in each image source for two reasons: (1) if Web visitors choose not to view graphic images, the alternative text will be shown; and (2) if visitors use Internet Explorer and leave the mouse over any graphic image, the text will be displayed in your ALT Attribute.

Altered States: The psychology of changes in perception and other states of consciousness, via external and internal stimulation.

Alternate World Disorder: The range of discomfort, from mild headaches and disorientation to nausea from VR (virtual reality or "barfogenic zone"). See also Simulator Sickness.

Alternative Space: Small-scale, independent organizations administered by artists for the exhibition of work that is often experimental and outside mainstream art movements.

Ambient Light: A technique for producing stereoscopic images; right- and left-eye view of images are printed in red and blue. Viewers wear 3D glasses with a red filter on one eye and blue on the other, which forces each eye to see different images causing the mind to build a 3D scene.

American Institute of Graphic Arts (AIGA): A New York-based organization that allows professionals to exchange ideas and information, participate in critical analysis and research, and advance education and ethical practice.

Analog Ripper: A piece of equipment that converts analog signals from cassette tapes, vinyl, or radio to WAV files. See also Ripping.

Analog Signal: A signal similar to or "analogous" to a physical process. Analog signals degrade when copied, modified, or transmitted. Analog electronic signals are distinguished from digital signals, which represent discrete numerical samples of information.

Analog: A form of measurement in which the indicator has no fixed state, such as ON and OFF. Analog also describes a wave that continuously varies in strength and quality.

Analog-to-Digital Converter (ADC): An electronic device used at the input of digital audio equipment to convert analog electrical signals to digital values whose numbers represent the level and frequency information contained in the original analog signal. To playback sound files, the sound card uses a DAC (Digital-to-Analog Converter). The ADC samples the audio at very fast intervals ("sampling rate"), producing a stream of snapshots. When played back by the DAC at the same pace, the samples are perceived as sound.

Anamorphic Lens: A special lens that enables a wide-screen picture to be shot on a smaller format film. The lens compresses, or "squeezes," the image vertically as it is photographed. A compatible lens on the projectory reverses the process, or expands the image, producing proportioned images.

Anchor: An area, in whole or part, within the content of a node that is the source or destination of a link. Typically, a mouse click on an anchor area redirects to its link, leaving the anchor at the end of the link displayed. Anchors tend to be highlighted or represented by a special symbol. Also known as Span, Region, Button, or Extent.

Animated GIF: A Graphics Interchange Format that consists of two or more GIFs shown in a timed sequence to give the effect of motion.

Animated Texture: A texture map replaced sequentially frame-by-frame to convey change or movement.

Animatic: A sequence of storyboard frames videotaped and edited for playback.

Animating: The act of imparting life to—making objects appear to move.

Animation Camera: A motion picture with single-frame and reverse capabilities for animation work, mounted on a crane over compound.

Animation Cel: A term categorized in two parts—production cels and limited edition cels. Also a painting on a clear sheet of acetate, usually 12.5 x 10.5 or larger. All cels are original paintings, not prints or reproductions.

Animation Director: A person responsible for supervising a team of animators, and for developing the behavior of all digital characters in a production.

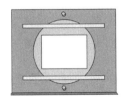

animation disc

Animation Disc: A steel or heavy aluminum disc mounted over circular table. A sheet of frosted plastic or glass is set into the disc, light from a fixture below the surface shines through the glass, enabling the animator to see his drawings through several sheets of paper at one time. Pegs are affixed to the disc to hold the drawing paper in register. Because the pegs hold the paper stationary, the disc rotates 360° enabling the animator to work at any angle.

Animation Drawing: Original rough drawings created by film animators from which the cels are traced or Xeroxed. "Experts" may argue that animation drawings represent the real art of an animated film. Also known as Pencil Drawing.

Animation Editor: A person who constructs the titles and credits for videos. Animation Editor is also an interactive software tool for the graphical specification, presentation, and modification of the values of animation parameters for computer facial models.

Animation Setup Technical Director (ASTD): A person who designs, creates, and provides support to controls that define how characters move and bend.

Animation Software: Software primarily used to create, edit, and animate GIFs.

Animation Stand: Adjustable structure that holds and controls camera and drawings (or objects) for creating animation.

Animation Supervisor: The person who supervises, checks, and corrects the key animators' drawings; often, but not always, the character designer as well.

Animation: The creation of a timed sequence, or series of graphic images or frames together to give the appearance of continuous movement. This creates the illusion of movement caused by rapid display of a series of still images.

Animator: An artist who uses frame-by-frame filmmaking techniques to give artwork the illusion of movement.

Animatronics: Robotics that simulate animal life; popular in film and museums.

Anime: Japanese animation style. Also referred to as Japanimation.

Anisotropic Filtering: A texture filtering method, specifically for non-square filtering, usually of textures shown in radical perspective (such as a pavement texture as seen from a camera lying on the road). More generally, anisotropic improves clarity of images with severely unequal aspect ratios.

Annotation: The linking of a new commentary node to an existing node. If readers can annotate nodes, they can immediately provide feedback if the information is misleading, out of date or incorrect, thus improving the quality of Web information.

Analog: Non-digital, non-computerize format. A manual format or linear format such as Analog Video, which is designed to play in a linear fashion from the first frame to the last. DVD is an example of digital format

Anonymous FTP: Internet File Transfer Protocol tool allowing connection to a site, the ability to search available files, and download any file, document, or program without having to establish a user-id and password on the specific system. By using the special user-id "anonymous," the network user will circumvent local security checks and have access to publicly accessible files on the remote system. Most systems that permit anonymous login require the user's email address as the password.

ANSI: See American National Standards Institute.

Answer Print: The first print of a film in release form, prepared by the laboratory for acceptance by the producer, then used as a standard for all subsequent prints.

Anti-aliasing: A software technique used to smooth edges where individual pixels are visible; used to smooth out image resolution artifacts such as "jaggies" by anticipating and displaying the interim pixels.

Anticipation: A pause or small countermove made by a character in preparation for a major movement; used by animators to give the illusion of body movement with the proper sense of weight and balance.

Aperture (Lens): This is the small hole that opens in the lens and directs the amount of light coming in contact with the film plane. As the Aperture or T-stop number increases the amount of light hitting the film through the gate decreases.

Aperture Plates: Mattes on a movie projector, manually adjustable.

Aperture Priority: A mode in which a desired lens opening (f-stop) is manually selected and locked in so camera can select appropriate shutter speed for proper exposure. Used primarily to control depth of field (range of sharpness) in front of or behind subject.

API (Application Programming Interface): Web server capability extensions used by programmers to write applications capable of interacting with other applications. See also Server API.

APL (A Programming Language): A programming language best known for its use of non-ASCII symbols, including a few Greek letters.

Apparent Surface Orientation: The orientation (direction) a surface appears to point in an image. It's controlled by the shading normal vector, not necessarily the same as the normal vector of the primitive as it's actually drawn (the geometric normal vector).

Applets: Small programs within application programs that produce various special effects. For example, WordArt, a Windows applet, lets you produce special effects with text. WordArt is invoked by selecting Insert from the menu.

Application Programming Interface: See API.

Applications: See Software Applications.

Armature: A joined, metal skeletal structure onto which the figure of an animated puppet is built, providing support and shape for the figure, as well as the ability to be properly manipulated.

dog armature

ARPANet: See Advanced Research Projects Agency.

Art Corner Setups: Cels, sold for a few dollars a piece, at Disneyland's Art Corner shop in Tomorrowland from 1955 to the late 60s. Setups were usually trimmed to fit a small mat, and included a litho background or sheet of colored paper, and a gold foil authenticating sticker on the back of the mat. Despite the quantities of Art Corner setups sold, decent poses continue to be in great demand with collectors.

Art Director: The person who oversees the creative direction of print graphics or art projects. The person who oversees the artists and craftspeople who build the movie sets as in a movie art director.

Art Technologique: Art that employs devices such as machines, rather than materials such as paint.

Article: A single message posted to a newsgroup. The term "article" is being replaced by "post" or "message."

Articulation: Objects composed of several parts that are separately moveable.

Artifacts: The flaws in the image due to the technical limitations of the computer or video device.

Artificial Intelligence (AI): The attempt to mimic and automate human cognitive skills through rules and knowledge representation techniques (i.e., understanding visual images, recognizing speech and written text, solving problems, making medical diagnoses, heuristic knowledge, etc.).

Artificial Life: Digital agents that evolve, reproduce, grow, and change in similar ways to biological life forms.

Artificial Reality: A term introduced by arts and computer visualization scholar Myron Krueger in the mid-1970s to describe his computer-generated responsive environments. Krueger has emphasized the non-intrusive (Second: Person VR) systems that track people with pattern recognition techniques then display them, and the surround, on projection systems (See CAVE). As realized in his Videoplace and the Vivid Group's Mandala system, it is a computer display system that perceives and captures "a participant's action in terms of the body's relationship to a graphic world and generates responses (usually imagery) that maintain the illusion that his actions are taking place within that world." See also Virtual Reality and Cyberspace.

ASCII (American Standard Code for Information Interchange): The standard character set of text files.

ASF (Active Streaming Format): The standard file format of Windows Media files.

ASIFA (Association Internationale du Film d'Animation): International Animated Film Association. A non-profit organization devoted to the advancement of the art of animation.

ASP (Active Server Pages): An open, compile-free application environment in which to combine HTML pages, scripts, and ActiveX server components.

Aspect Ratio: The height-to-width ratio of an image. For example, the standard TV frame is 4:3; the relationship between the width (length) and the height of the film format; the classic film ratio, a format seen in 35mm in the Academy Aperture, was 4:3 or 1.33:1, which was adopted by television. Wide-aspect ratios include VistaVision (1.5:1) and Cinemascope (2:33:1). High Definition Television offers a 16:9 or 1.77:1 aspect ratio. In computer graphics, aspect ratio refers to the relationship of width-to-height of the horizon and vertical pixels.

Aspherical Lens: A lens designed to better reproduce images by having its edges flattened so that it is not a perfect sphere, hence: "a" (not) "spherical" (a sphere).

Assembler: A low-level computer language used to execute high-speed events**.**

Assistant Director (AD): Assistant to the director. See also Director.

ASTD: See Animation Setup Technical Director.

ASX: Windows Media reference file placed on the HTTP server that gives Media Player the location of the ASF file on the NetShow server; may contain references to multiple movies, different content locations, or temporal aspects.

Asymmetric Digital Subscriber Line (ADSL): A DSL that sends data quickly downstream (to you) but upstream slowly, allocating the digital resources of the twisted pair efficiently for many download-heavy applications.

Asymmetric Digital Subscriber Line: See ADSL.

Asynchronous Communication: Users communicating at different times.

Atmospheric Effects: A term that refers to two other effects that form an atmospheric effect when they are combined. For example, fogging and depth cueing.

Attachment: Any file linked to an email message that can be opened and viewed by a recipient's computer.

Attenuation: The total or partial reduction of signal levels.

Attenuation Threshold: Suppressing sound above a certain level.

Attraction Loop: An eye-catching opening sequence for a new media presentation that will cycle until stopped by user response. Most often found in kiosk applications.

Attributes: Characteristics of models, cameras, and lights.

Audio CD Tracks: Individual songs or cuts on an audio CD (compact disc).

Audio Conference: A telephone meeting with participants in different geographic locations speaking to one another simultaneously.

Audio Graphics: A hardware and software system that permits computer users in different locations to connect via telephone lines to share data, graphics, and audio information.

Audio Interchange File Format: See AIFF.

Audio Layback: After editing video footage, audio is recorded back onto the picture to be in synch with the actor's lines.

Audio Scrubbing: The process of movement within an audio file or tape to locate a particular section. The term originally comes from the days of reel-to-reel players, when rocking a reel would give the impression of scrubbing tape across the head. Many audio scrub tools today allow the user to drag a cursor across the waveform to audition different sections of an audio file.

Audio Sweetening: Adjusting sound levels of a certain section of a track on a sound mix; minor adjustments of mixing soundtracks can make major improvements in the quality of the complete audio.

Audio Video Interleaved (AVI): Digital video architecture for use in Microsoft Windows, common standard for synchronized audio/video delivery on IMC-compatible computers. Blocks of audio data are woven into a stream of video frames.

Audio Visual: See AV.

Audio: A term used to describe anything related to sound, as in audiotape, audio track, or audio file.

Augmented Reality: The use of transparent displays worn as glasses on which data can be projected, allowing the repair of radar, for example, and having the needed data displayed on the glasses while circling the radar.

Authoring Software: Programs used to create full, multimedia productions, such as simulations and tutorials. Although most of these programs have some point-and-click features to simplify development, most require some knowledge of programming language concepts.

Authoring: A term used to describe the process of writing a document. "Authoring" seems to have come into use in order to emphasize that document production involves more than just writing.

Auto CAD: A general-purpose computer-aided drafting application program designed for use on single-user desktops. See also CAD.

Autofocus: A camera function to automatically focus on the subject it is pointed toward.

Automatic Dialog Replacement (ADR): Re-recording of dialog by actors in a sound studio during post-production, usually performed to playback of edited picture in order to match lip movements on screen.

Automatic Dialog Replacement Editing: The process of editing sound during Automatic Dialog Replacement.

Automatic Dialog Replacement Editor: The person who performs ADR editing.

Automatic Gain Control (AGC): Circuitry used to ensure that output signals are maintained at constant levels in the face of widely varying input signal levels. AGC is typically used to maintain a constant video luminance level by boosting weak (low light) picture signals electronically. Some equipment include gain controls which are switchable between automatic and manual control.

Automatic Playlist: A playlist created by specifying the length of the playlist desired, and defining the types of music desired.

Autotracing: The process of converting a bit-mapped image (or raster image) into a vector image. In a bit-mapped image, each object is represented by a pattern of dots. In a vector image, every object is defined geometrically.

AV (Audio Visual): The making use of or relating to both hearing and sight and to electronic media in general.

Avatar: One's likeness, image, or puppet in the VR.

Average Blending: When using texture blending, this term refers to the average colors of the base and the light maps when blended together evenly.

AVI: See Audio Video Interleave.

AVID: Servers, networks, and media tools created by Avid Technology Inc—a recognized digital standard for media professionals.

AVR: Sound format created by Audio Visual Research used on Atari ST computers.

AWK: Aho, Weinberger and Kaho, the last names of AWK's authors. A command language allowing users to manipulate files containing columns of data and strings.

Azimuth: Defined by projecting the angle of the sun onto the X-axis (horizontal).

B

Back Lights: The process of lighting a subject from behind, or from the opposite side to the camera, to create a silhouette of the subject.

Back Link: A link in one direction implied from the existence of an explicit link in the opposite direction.

Back Porch: The portion of the video waveform between the trailing edge of the horizontal sync and the start of active video.

Backbone: The primary trunk or high-speed connection within a network that connects shorter, often slower circuits or LANs. It carries the heaviest traffic and is central to any network design.

Back-End Team: This term includes database administrators, system engineers, business analysts, and systems administrators.

Backface Culling: The process of removing unseen polygons that face away from the viewer, dramatically speeding up the rendering of a polygonal scene by using valuable processing power. Also known as Backface Removal or Back Culling.

Backface Removal: The elimination of polygons that face away from the viewer. See also Backface Culling.

Background Drawing or Layout: A sketch used as the basis for a background painting with the placement and action of the characters in that scene, occasionally with color highlights. Drawings or layouts may show proposed action of animated characters with characters roughly drawn in blue or red pencil.

Background Painting: The artwork, usually a painting, upon which the cels are overlaid to be photographed for a film. A feature-length film will require about 1,000 backgrounds because many cels can be photographed over one background. Therefore, backgrounds are rare and a set-up including a cel and its matching background is much more valuable than the price of the cel alone.

Background Projection: See Rear Projection.

Background: The screen area or frame behind images or objects, the most distant element in composite layering. The background may also be a flat piece of artwork that serves as the setting for the animated action, and which may vary from a realistically rendered scene to a sheet of colored paper.

Backlight Switch: Camera control which overrides auto iris system and opens the iris two or three F-stops. Commonly used in backlit situations where auto-iris would result in dark skin tones and underexposure.

Backlit Animation: A form of animation in which partly transparent art work is lit from behind. This technique was traditionally used to create a kind of neon glow effect as seen in the feature move Tron.

Backstory: All information about the character, and his/her relationships to other characters, that takes place before the story begins.

Backup: The act of creating an archival copy of data recorded on a storage medium.

Backwards: The direction of tracing from the camera to the light source.

Bandpass Filter: A circuit that allows only a selected range of frequencies to pass through.

Bandwidth: The amount of data, measured usually in bits per second that can be sent through a dedicated (leased) transmission circuit.

Bank: Simultaneously rolling and translating the camera in the same direction.

Banner: A graphic image (static, animated, or rich media) that is placed on Websites as an advertisement; commonly used for brand awareness and generating sales.

Bar Code: A pattern of parallel lines whose variable thickness and separation encode a message that can be read by an optical scanner or wand for decoding by a computer.

Bar Sheet: A printed form, used by directors and animators in planning the movement of art and camera, on which all elements of a film (including music, voice, sound effects, visuals) are charted frame-by-frame in their relationship to time.

Barrel Distortion: The opposite of pin-cushioning in a video display where vertical sides of the display area curve outwards.

Base Map: When using texture blending, this is the term used to describe the main texture used on the polygon. One or more additional textures are blended with the base map to create a new texture. See also Dark Map, Light Map.

Base Multitimbral Specification: A synthesizer subsystem standard that Multimedia PC audio-board manufacturers follow in implementing MIDI playback.

Baseband: An audio or video signal that is not modulated onto another carrier (such as RF modulated to channel 3 or 4). In DTV, baseband also may refer to the basic (unaltered) MPEG 2 program or system stream.

BASIC (Beginners' All-purpose Symbolic Instruction Code): An algebraic computer programming language developed at Dartmouth College, Hanover, N.H. The language employs if/then-type logic statements, and other English commands, as well as mathematical formulas.

Batch Compression: The grouping two or more movies together to be compressed sequentially, so that compressions do not need to be started manually.

Batch File: Used in MS-DOS, this is a text-based file using the file extension .bat that carries out commands when executed.

Batch List: The specific list of movies to be compressed in a batch, as well as the settings with which each movie will be processed.

Baud: A unit of transmission speed named for Jean-Maurice-Emile Baudo that defines the number of discrete signaling elements per second. Common baud rates are 300, 1200, 2400, 9600, 14 400, and 28 800 bits per seconds (bps).

Bay: In the physical frame of a microcomputer case, this is a space where an internal drive or a peripheral is installed.

Beam Current: The current of an electron beam in a cathode ray tube. The current is the number of electrons per unit time, which is usually measured in milliamperes. A higher beam current produces a brighter phosphor dot.

Beat outline: The fourth phase of the animation process, it is not always a required step; it includes a specific breakdown of the story's action and gag sequences.

Beginning of the Story: The part of a story that usually introduces the main characters, establishes the dramatic premise, and sets up the event situations that will develop the story.

Benchmark: A task or series of tasks used to test capabilities of a processor or system.

Bendy Box: 3D shape-deformation controllers used in most animation software.

Beta: The second letter of the Greek alphabet. In software development, a beta test is the second phase of software testing in which a sampling of the intended audience tries the product out.

Bevel: This gives an image a raised appearance by applying highlighted colors and shadows to the inner and outer edges.

Beveling: Works by truncating the hard edge between adjacent surfaces and replacing it with a slanted plane.

Bezel: The housing that encases the front of a video monitor.

Bézier Curve: This curve passes through all of its control points.

Bézier Spline: Named after French Mathematician Pierre Bézier (pronounced BEZ-ee-ay), this is a term that describes curves which interpolate between two endpoints, with additional parameters governing the shape determined by two "control points." This type of curve is used, for example, in drawing scalable fonts. Also called B-Spline Curves.

B-Frame: A MPEG difference frame based on both the previous and next frames. Similar to a QuickTime delta frame, plus the ability to see what's ahead. Also known as Bi-directional Frame.

Bilinear Filtering: A means of predicting the most appropriate texture pixel for the screen based on interpolation from the four adjacent pixels in the texture.

Billboard: A texture that always maintains its alignment to the viewer, and is often scaled up and down to place it in a 3D scene.

Binary: Having only two states, ON and OFF, or 0 and 1.

Binary File: A file that can only be read with special software, such as word processors or image viewers; contain special, embedded codes (i.e., program commands) that create bold or underlined text, for example.

Binary Large Object: See BLOB.

Binary Space Partition: See BSP.

Binary System: A system based on only two numbers, 0 and 1, unlike the decimal system, which is based on numbers from 0 through 9. Consider the binary system to be based on powers of two, and the decimal system to be based on powers of 10, because in the binary system one adds another number place every time another power of two is reached (2,4,8,etc), and in the decimal system one adds another place every time a power of 10 (10,100,1000) is reached.

Binary Transfer: A method of transferring information between computers that involves the use of error-correction protocol.

Binaural Audio: Two audio tracks that are recorded with special microphone placement for each track to provide listeners with the perception of depth, or 3D sound, when tracks are played back together.

Binocular Omni-orientation Monitor: See Boom.

Bioinformatics: The application of computer technology to the management of biological information. Specifically, it is the science of developing computer databases and algorithms to facilitate and expedite biological research. The Human Genome Project is using Bioinformatics largely in the field of human genome research, which has been determining the sequence of the entire human genome (about 3 billion base pairs) and is essential in using genomic information to understand diseases. It is also used largely for the identification of new molecular targets for drug discovery.

Biosensors: Special glasses or bracelets containing electrodes to monitor muscle electrical activity. For example, tracking eye movements by measuring muscle movements.

Biotechnics: Art that combines biology with technology.

Bipack Camera: A camera equipped with twin sets of magazines and able to run two strips of film simultaneously.

Bipack Printing: The use of a Bipack Camera as a contact film printer. Such a printer can be used to generate composite images, combining, for example mat painting with live-action plate shot earlier and elsewhere.

Bit: A binary unit of storage that can represent only one of two values, ON and OFF, or 0 and 1 (binary digit).

Bit Block Transfer: A transformation of a rectangular block of pixels. Typical transformations include changing the color or shade of all pixels or rotating the entire rectangle. Many modern video adapters include hardwired bit block transformations, which execute much faster than when executed by software routines.

Bit Depth: The amount of color data, expressed in number of bits, that is available by a system; i.e. 8-bits allows a maximum 256 levels of information to be represented for each component (Y,R-Y,B-Y). Bit depth affects the size of the file and the resultant resolution or image quality.

Bitmap (BMP): A collection of pixels that describes an image as a complete picture, can be of various bit depth and resolution. Bitmap is also an array of pixels.

Bitmap Image: A graphic image stored as a specific arrangement of screen dots or pixels. Web graphics are bitmap images. This term also describes a graphic defined by specifying the colors of dots or pixels that make up the picture; common types of bitmap graphics are GIF, JPEG, Photoshop, PCX, TIFF, Macintosh or Microsoft Paint, BMP, PNG, FAX formats, and TGA. Also known as Raster Graphics.

Black Box: An electronic circuit or assembly that can be isolated from a system in order to perform a special function, such as controlling an external peripheral.

Black Level: Represents the darkest an image can be made, defining the level of black for video systems. If the video descends below this level it is referred to as blacker-than-black. For example, sync is blacker-than-black.

Black Limbo: The environment created when a set is covered with non-reflective black material so that the actors or miniatures placed in it will stand out as elements that can easily be isolated. White limbo is also used the same end.

Blanking: The time period of a video display electron beam when turned off then reset to its position of the next scan line.

BLOB (Binary Large Object): A collection of binary data stored as a single entity in a database management system (DBMS). It is used primarily to hold multimedia objects such as images, videos and sound, though they can also be used to store programs or fragments of code. Not all DBMSs support BLOBs.

Blobby Surface: Surfaces that are dynamic and constantly regenerated as they move in and out of the areas of influence of blobby elements.

Blue Screen: An image that starts with a subject that has been photographed in front of an evenly lit, bright, pure blue background. The composition process, whether photographic or electronic, replaces all the blue in the picture with another image, known as the background plate; can be made optically for still photos or movies, electronically for live video, and digitally to computer images. Other colors can be used, green is the most common, although sometimes red has been used for special purposes.

Blurring Filter: A special-effects filter that stimulates an out-of-focus photograph.

BMP: See Bitmap Image.

Body English: The involuntary movements made by people while talking. Also known as Body Language.

Body Suit: Full-body-covering clothing interfaced to a computer system allowing the wearer to interact with cyberspace.

Bones: Individual components of a skeleton animation system.

Bookmark: Electronic bookmarks are used to link to a Website you may want to return to. Netscape lets you bookmark any site then save the bookmarks in a file to be recalled at any time. Microsoft Internet Explorer uses the term "favorite," rather than bookmark, for the same concept.

Boolean: A function in 3D modeling that allows for the creation of negative space, such as finger holes in a bowling

---

ball. Boolean union, Boolean intersection, and Boolean difference are common commands in high-end 3D packages.

Boolean Operations: In order to create a Boolean object, you first need two other objects, which can be primitives or other meshes. They also need to intersect in 3D space. When referring to addition, the resulting object will be the sum of the two initial objects. It will look as if the two were welded. When referring to subtraction, the second object will be subtracted from the first. A hole in the shape of the second object is created in the first. All space that was occupied by both objects is taken away from the first. In the intersection mode, the final object occupies the area in which both initially intersected.

BOOM (Binocular Omni-orientation Monitor): A 3D display device suspended from a weighted boom that can swivel freely about so the viewer doesn't have to wear an HMD—instead, it steps up to the viewer like a pair of binoculars. The boom's position communicates the user's point of view to the computer.

Bootleg Recording: The unauthorized recording of a live concert, CD, cassette tape, record album, or musical broadcast on radio or television. Also known as Pirate or Underground Recording.

Bottlenecks: The points in a system that is slower than the rest of the system, causing overall delays. On the Internet, bottlenecks are often caused by localized problems, such as overloaded switching complexes or slow modems.

Bottom Lighting: A term that refers to when the source of illumination for photographing a scene comes from beneath the artwork.

Boundary Modeling Technique: This technique focuses on the shell of objects and ignores the volume and inner structure.

Bounding Box: A square box created by clicking and dragging; often used in graphical user interfaces to select an object or group of objects on the screen. These are defined by the points most distant from the center of the model.

BPC: Bits Per Channel.

BPI: Bits Per Inch.

Branch: To leap from one program location to another based on programmed responses to user input.

Branching Point: An optional path that a user may choose given two or more directions or destinations.

Breaking The Fourth Wall: A term that refers to when a character turns and speaks directly into the camera to the audience.

Breezeway: A portion of the video waveform between the trailing edge of horizontal sync and the start of color burst.

Brightness: A component file of the HSB (Hue, Saturation, and Brightness) color model. For RGB (Red, Green, and Blue) pixels, the largest component value is the brightness.

Broadcast: A term that refers to signals intended for delivery via the television system, as well as network delivery to a wide audience.

Broadcaster Relatable: A term that refers to when a story does not break any of the specific broadcaster's guidelines in regards to safety and legality.

Broken Hierarchy: A term that refers to when some or all of the limbs do not descend from the chain root, but instead have their own root.

Browser: Software used to view, manage, and access Web pages by interpreting hypertext and hyperlinks. The two most common browsers are Netscape and Microsoft Internet Explorer. Web pages often appear differently depending on the brand and version of the browser.

BSP (Binary Space Partition): A data structure commonly used for computer graphics and other geometric searching problems. Formed by cutting space by a hyperplane then recursively partitioning each of the two resulting half-spaces. The result is a hierarchical decomposition of space into convex cells.

B-Spline: The process of making a curved line with few points. Have control points with equal weights to adjust the shape of the curve. Control points rarely reside on the curve because it is an average of the points. For example, when making four control points in the shape of a square, the resulting curve will be a circle inside the square because the curve is pulled inward as it tries to average the weights of all four points.

Bucket: Subportion of a final rendered image's frame buffer devoted to rendering as one unit.

Buffer Memory: Space that temporarily stores a small amount of data to help compensate for differences in the transfer rate of data from one device to another.

Buffer: A temporary electronic storage area where several already-exposed digicam images can wait in line to be processed. This speeds the interval between shots because each photo does not have to be processed before the next can be taken.

Bug: An error in a computer program or a problem with the system.

Build: An interim version of software in which bugs are resolved and features are refined prior to release.

Build-up: The sequential construction of your story that builds tension and suspense through its action and/or comedy.

Bump Mapping: Used to add detail to an image without increasing the number of polygons. It relies on light-reflection calculations to create small bumps on the surface of the object in order to give it texture; the surface of the object is not changed. Bumps are applied by matching up a series of grayscale pixels with colored pixels on the rendered, colored object. Lighter grayscale pixels create a sense of maximum relief or maximum indentation, while darker pixels have less effect.

Burn: The act of changing a text or sprite track into an image in the video track.

Burning: The process of writing information to a CD. A tern also used to describe the darkening specific areas of an image.

Burn-on-Demand: Creating an audio CD in response to a customer's request for specific tracks.

Byte: A unit of storage composed of eight bits. It can store a numeric value from 0 to 255 (decimal) or one letter. See also BIT.

C

C++: A popular object-oriented computer-programming language.

C Language: C is a structured, procedural programming language that has been widely used both for operating systems and applications and that has had a wide following in the animation community.

CAD: Computer-aided design or Computer-assisted design.

Calibration: The setting or correcting of a measuring device or base level, usually by adjusting it to match or conform to a dependably known and unvarying measure. For example, the brightness or black level of a video display can be calibrated using a PLUGE pattern.

CAM: Computer-Aided Manufacturing.

Camcorder: Combination of camera and videotape recorder in one device. Camcorders permit easy and rapid photography and recording simultaneously. Camcorders are available in most home video formats: 8mm, Hi-8, VHS, VHS-C, S-VHS, etc.

Camera Blocking: The process of notating the changing position of the camera, lens size, and focus during a particular scene.

Camera Field: The area being photographed by the camera.

Camera Operator: The person responsible for translating the instructions on the script.

Camera: Serves as an object to view other objects of a scene.

Canvas Size: The full editable area of an image.

Capping: This term determines whether the round sides of the cones or cylinders are open or closed.

Capture: The term for "recording" audio or video from an analog source (like VHS tape) to a digital format (a file).

Cartesian Coordinate System: Developed by Rene Descartes, this system labels the three axes as X, Y, and Z.

Cartoon Bible: A document of 30-45 pages of written information on the cartoon series. It includes character descriptions and relationships, sample springboards, any myths or legends that set up the cartoon, a summary of the series, and descriptions of the sets and locations.

Cartoon Lineage: A "family" link from a classic cartoon character to a new one.

Cartoon Physical Feats: Feats performed by cartoon characters which defy the laws of the universe and which humans cannot perform without grave consequences.

Cartoon Tunnel: The genre of a cartoon.

Cartoonist: The professional title given to a person who draws cartoons, often for comic strips or caricatures.

Cartooniverse: The world in which the cartoon characters live.

Cascading Style Sheets (CSS): A mechanism that allows authors and readers to attach the same style (i.e. fonts, colors and spacing) to multiple HTML documents. The CSS1 language is human readable and writable, and expresses style in common desktop publishing terminology.

Casein-Based Cel Paints: In an effort to lower production costs, some studios, most notably the Warner Brothers cartoon studio, used a casein-based paint. Made from dairy curd, this binder adhered well to the cel stock for the short term, but its high level of acidity and its tendency to become severely dehydrated made it very unstable over the long term. Almost every cel painted with this type of paint at the Warner's Studio has cracked and chipped over time.

Cast Shadow: Similar to a drop shadow with added emphasis on perspective. It can be rotated, stretched, and skewed to create a realistic 3D effect.

Casting: The assignment of dramatic roles to actors.

Cathode Ray Tube (CRT): A television picture tube. The cathode ray excites the pixels to create the video image.

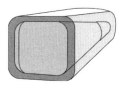

CRT display

CAVE: VR using projection devices used on the walls and ceiling to give the illusion of immersion.

CCD: See Charge Coupled Device.

CCIR-601: The international standard for conversion of analog video to digital video, now identified as ITU-R-601. ITU-R-601 specifies 720 samples per line, yielding a frame size of 720x480 (NTSC) or 720x576 (PAL). ITU-R-601 is the international standard for professional video applications.

CCITT V Series: Several international modem standards set by the Consultative Committee for International Telephony and Telegraphy, which help buyers to be sure modems will communicate with other modems. The standards, formerly used primarily outside the United States, have been accepted almost universally since the advent of the 2400 bits per second (bps) modems. Not all are relevant to computer users. Examples include: V.21, V.22, V.22bis, V.23, V.26, V.26bis, V.27, V.27bis, V.27ter, V.29, V.32, V.32bis, V.34, V.42, V.42bis.

CD (Compact Disk): These audio CDs hold about one hour of music. Digital CDs (Also known as CD-ROMs) hold up to 650MB of information.

CD-DA Files: Individual songs or cuts on a CD. Note: there is actually just CD-DA: Compact Disc Digital Audio. Also known as Raw WAV Files.

CD-i (Compact Disc Interactive): An extension of the CD format designed around a set-top computer that connects to a TV to provide interactive home entertainment, including digital audio and video, video games, and software applications. Defined by the Green Book standard.

CD-R (Compact Disc, Recordable): Refers to compact disc that can be recorded one at a time, or the equipment used to make the recordings. The CD-R disc can only be recorded once; if the recorded content is no longer wanted, additional material can be recorded only on the space remaining subject to the recording method chosen. If there is no remaining space the disc is not recordable. The disc themselves are constructed differently from ordinary non-recordable CD's.

CD-R Burner: A device that uses a blank CD that can't be reused or reburned. Also known as CD-ROM Burner.

CD-R/E: Compact Disc, Recordable/Erasable.

CD-ROM "hybrids": CD-ROMs with embedded Internet links. Although the Web can provide current information, for example, timely updates and corrections, it lacks the bandwidth to deliver large multimedia files quickly. The "Internet-enabled" CD-ROM, or "cybrid," is being touted as a software tool that will use the strengths of both technologies. The parts of a program that can slow down access time if downloaded from the Internet (multimedia, index searches) are kept on the CD-ROM for faster loading. The Internet side of the equation is used for providing and adding new features without having to send out a new CD-ROM disc. In the near future, look for hybrid DVDs.

CD-ROM (Compact Disc Read-Only Memory): Identical in size and shape to an audio/music CD, but organized to store computer data rather than sound. A single CD-ROM disc can hold more than 600MB of information, equivalent to 428 floppy disks. CD-ROM drives are now multi-session, reading information 2x, 4x, 6x, 8x, and 10x faster than original music CD players. Computer CD-ROM drives can slow down to single-speed to play music CDs.

CD-ROM Servers: Devices such as towers, changers, and jukeboxes that allow you to put CD-ROMs on networks: one CD, rather than multiple copies, serves many users. CD-ROM towers stack multiple drives, sometimes as many as 40, in a single box. Each drive has a read head for its CD, providing fast access. CD-ROM changers swap CDs in and out of the ONE drive. The jukebox, the changer's "big brother," can store up to 2,000 CDs and can be as big as a refrigerator. The swapping action can slow CD access, especially for changers.

CD-RW (Compact Disc, Rewritable): Refers to compact discs that can be recorded one a time and where an unwanted recording can be recorded over. The discs themselves are constructed differently from other types of CD's; they contain an organic dye that represents the pits that in turn represent the recorded content. Not all CD players can play CD-RW disks since the reflective surface has a different color from the usual silver or gold.

CD-RW Burner: A CD-ROM writing device that uses a reusable CD, allowing one to write data to it, use it like any other CD, and then erase it and write new information.

Cel: A sheet of clear plastic (celluloid or cellulose), which contains the characters that are placed over a background. These are then photographed in succession, and together they comprise the action of an animated film. The outline of the image, whether hand-inked or xeroxed, is applied to the front of the cel. The vivid colors that bring the character(s) to life are then hand painted onto the rear of the cel. Occasionally, certain dark colors are painted onto the front to reduce glare. The cels are laid over a background and filmed in succession comprising the action of an animated film.

Cel Animation: A term used to describe traditional animation. Figures are drawn and transferred onto cels, painted, then placed over a background, and photographed frame by frame. Often referred to as Disney style animation as it is the most common style used by early Walt Disney Company.

Cel Levels: The number of cels that have been combined to make one complete action frame.

Cel Setup: A combination of a cel or cels with some sort of background, whether matching or not. These might have as many as 10 cel layers placed atop one another to achieve an effect.

Celestial Bodies: These bodies usually move very slowly because the light sources are distant.

Celluloid: Clear acetate on which traditional animation is inked and painted.

Cellulose Acetate: The material used to make a cel. It is much more stable material than cellulose nitrate and is currently used for cel production.

Cellulose Nitrate: The material used for cels from the 1920s to 1950s. Nitrate cels usually show signs of yellowing, shrinkage, and warping or ripping. This material was discontinued because it was considered highly combustible.

Central Question Avenue: The question that spins the story and which is answered in the climax.

CFML (Cold Fusion Markup Language; an extension of HTML): A proprietary markup language used by Allaire's Cold Fusion to link HTML pages to database servers; fills some important gaps in HTML, including session variables, branching logic, loops and other constructs that programmers are accustomed to using, such as error trapping and debugging tools.

CGATS: Committee for Graphics Arts Technologies Standards.

CGI: See Computer-generated Imagery.

Chain Root: The first joint in the first segment of an articulated chain.

Channel: One piece of information stored with an image. True color images, for instance, have three channels: red, green, and blue.

Channel-Casting: This technology publishes/broadcasts personalized information to subscribers, then, rather than using bookmarks and search engines to pull down information, users run a client application updated with data that is "pushed" down by a server. Also known as Push Technology or Web-Casting.

Character: A personality that is given to an animated object.

Character Animation: The art of making an animated figure move like a unique individual—the creation of living characters, either by traditionally or computer-generated animation.

Character Arc: The learning curve of a character. It's what a character learns in the course of the story, although, in animation it will not change the character generally.

Character Compass: The major and minor character traits that establish a character's personality, including positive and negative traits.

Character Designs: The preliminary drawings of the characters done early in production.

Character Dipstick: A list of important moments in a character's life, and how they shaped his/her personality. It also includes any important relationship(s) which shapes/ has shaped the character, his backstory, and his physical traits.

Character Measurements: Measured in inches from the highest to the lowest point on the image.

Character Models: Standardized renderings of characters, expressions, props, and costumes. Character designs would be created by concept artists or lead animators, and when approved, photographic stats, called model sheets, would be produced and distributed to the various departments ensuring absolute consistency between the sketches of all of the artists working on a project.

Character Set-ups: The rigging or designing of skeleton and parameters to determine the character's range of motion.

Character Sheets: Drawings used to define primary emotions and attitudes of characters in the form of body positions and facial expressions.

Character Tag: The unique description of a character, used only when introducing a new character.

Character Tic: A trait or distinction given only to one particular character.

Charge Coupled Device (CCD): A special light-sensitive memory chip. The results convert to electrical impulses.

Check Box: Used to make selections in online forms.

Checker: A person who makes a dry run of a scene that is ready for the camera— the purpose is to detect and correct errors.

Checking: The step in production in which all elements of a scene are examined and checked against the exposure sheet to ensure they are correct before being filmed.

Children: Objects below the parent.

Chipping & Paint Loss: A portion of paint, from a small chip to an entire section, which has separated completely from the cel.

Chroma Bandpass: In a NTSC or PAL video signal, the luma (black-and-white) and the chroma (color) information are combined together. This filter removes the luma from the video signal, leaving the chroma relatively intact.

Chroma Key: A video system for replacing a specific color with another image. For example, in a newscast, a chroma keyer can be adjusted to detect the color of a blue screen, then placing the news announcer in front of another image.

Chrominance: The color component of an image.

Chrominance Signal: The portion of the composite video signal that contains the color information. This information describes hue and saturation.

CIE Color Space: A useful aid for understanding which colors can be seen.

CIF (Common Interchange Format): The Common Interface Format was developed to support video conferencing. It has an active resolution of 352 x 288 and a refresh rate of 29.97 frames per second.

Cinemascope: A very wide (2.21:1) aspect ratio, which is one of the standards in MPEG-2. When displayed on a normal television, Cinemascope material requires pronounced "letterboxing" (black bars on top and bottom).

Cinepak: A commonly used QuickTime codec for compression of video files on CD-ROM. Cinipak offers temporal and spatial compression, and data-rate limiting.

Circles: 2D, closed contours that require a radius or diameter, a number of control points, and a type of spline.

Circuit Board: An electronic board on which computer chips have been laminated. Also known as Printed Circuit Board (PCB).

City Block: A story sequence composed of 10-20 streets, or scenes, with its own beginning, middle and end, and obstacles or dilemmas that confront the driver.

CIX (Commercial Internet Exchange): A pact between network providers allowing accounting for commercial traffic.

Clay Animation: An animation technique involving the use of pliable clay figures that are manipulated before each exposure. Also known as Claymation.

Clay Animator: An animator that works with clay as a primary medium for creating stop-motion or frame-by-frame recorded animation.

Claymation: A term used to describe a stop-motion animation done through the use of sculpted clay. Animator Will Vinton is credited for creating this word. Gumby is one of the most popular examples of this form of animation.

Clean Up Drawing: A drawing done by referring to the rough drawing from which cels are created.

Clean Up: The process of retracing the animator's rough, sketchy drawings and converting them into finished drawings with smooth outlines.

Cliché: Phrases heard so often they become trite. An animation storyline that is predictable.

Click: To press and release a mouse button rapidly, usually over a hot spot or icon on the screen, in a graphical user interface (GUI).

Click Track: A timing device used when elements of the soundtrack are added after the animation has been completed. The beat to which the animation is matched is recorded onto tape and played through earphones for the conductor, sound effects creator, and/or voice artists, enabling them to match their sounds to the film.

Client/Server: A set of computer applications (programs) in which two or more computers work together. Server(s) store data and programs, which they deliver on request to clients. The interaction between the client and server occurs in the background, so users are typically unaware which computer handles what.

Climax: The dramatic clash or confrontation that occurs at the end of the story.

Clip: A form of cropping; the clipped region need not be rectangular.

Clip Art: Collections of pictures/photographs. Many application programs, such as PowerPoint, contain built-in clipart resources. Clip Art is also illustrations or artwork files that are made available for use in productions and projects.

Clip Audio: Collections of royalty-free sounds, including effects, voice clips, and music. Also known as Audio Clip.

Clip Video: Collections of royalty-free video. Also known as Video Clip.

Clipboard: A temporary storage location. Upon use of the Cut or Copy commands, the data is stored in the Clipboard.

Clipping Plane: Throws away polygons on the other side of itself. This can dramatically speed up the rendering of a polygonal scene, since unneeded polygons can take up valuable processing power.

Clone: The digital copy of a digital tape indistinguishable from the master.

Clone Tool: A popular tool in image editing programs that allows the copying of small groups of pixels from one location to another.

Cluster Animation: A method to shape interpolation by dividing the object's surface into groups and animating them; these groups are often called clusters.

CLUT: See Color Lookup Table.

CMOS (Complimentary Metal Oxide Semiconductor): Used in some digicams instead of CCDs because they have low power requirements and are less expensive.

CMYK (Cyan, Magenta, Yellow, and Black): The four colors used for color printing. The most acceptable format used to separate color images for printing.

CMYK Image: A four-channel image containing cyan, magenta, yellow, and black channels; a CMYK image is generally used to print a color separation.

Code: A set of rules.

CODEC (Coder-Decoder): A device that converts analog video and audio signals into a digital format for transmission over telecommunications facilities and also converts received digital signals back into analog format.

Cold Fusion: A popular and sophisticated set of products for building Websites and serving pages to users.

Cold Fusion Markup Language: See CFML.

Collaboration: Working together.

Collision Detection: Detects when points from two different surfaces occupy the same space.

Color Cast: Color cast changes the hue (color) of a selected part of an image while keeping the saturation and brightness intact. Viewing an image with a color cast can be similar to viewing it through colored lenses on eyeglasses. A commonly known color cast (in graphic design) is a duotone.

Color Correction: The process of correcting or enhancing the color of an image. Also the ability to correct color errors and change colors for aesthetic purposes, done either during the film-to-tape transfer or as a tape-to-tape process.

Color Depth: The amount of color stored in an image expressed in bits. An image with a 24-bit color depth can have 16.7 million colors.

Color Index Value: The input value to a color lookup table (LUT) of a display controller's video backend operating in pseudo color mode. Color index values are also referred to as pseudo colors.

Color Killer: A circuit that shuts off the color decoding if the incoming video does not contain color information. It looks for the color burst and if it isn't found, it shuts off the color decoding.

Color Look Up Table (CLUT): A table that establishes a correspondence between the global palette (64K colors, for example) and the subset of colors (the limited palette—made of 16 or 256 colors) used by a particular texture.

Color Maps: Used to compute the color of light reflected by the 3D surface in which the color map has been placed.

Color Model: A representative drawing or cel of a character, with all of the colors labeled, that serves as a reference for the painters.

Color Model Cel: Used to reference a character's colors. Often the colors are labeled directly on the cel or on a background cel. Also known as Inspirational Drawing.

Color Palette: Available color selections, ranging from 16 colors to 16.7 million; Macintosh and Windows share only 216 out of 256 colors. See also Dithering.

Color Perception: The sensation of hues created by the human eye as it defines the frequencies of electromagnetic waves.

Color Proof: A representation of the final printed product created to check color accuracy and other elements.

Color Purity: A term used to describe how close a color is to the theoretical. For example, in the YUV color space, color purity is specified as a percentage of saturation and +/-q, where q is an angle in degrees, and both quantities are referenced to the color of interest. The smaller the numbers, the closer the actual color is to the color that it's really supposed to be. For a studio-grade device, the saturation is +/-2% and the hue is +/-2 degrees. On a vectorscope, if you're in that range, you're at studio quality.

Color Separation: A color image that has been separated into the four process colors (CMYK).

Color Shifting: Occurs when a computer-generated image is moved from an additive color environment.

Color Space: A mathematical model describing colors. Common models include RGB, CMYK, HSV, and YUV.

Color Subsampling: A method of reducing the size of an image by storing color data with lower resolution than luminance data; typically used in video with the YUV color space; common subsampling options include 4:2:2, 4:1:1, and YUV9.

Color Temperature: Color temperature is measured in degrees Kelvin. If a TV has a color temperature of 8,000 degrees Kelvin, that means the whites have the same shade as a piece of pure carbon heated to that temperature. Low-color temperatures shift towards red; high-color temperatures shift towards blue.

Color Test: The footage of a film that has been timed and viewed to make sure that colors, characters and backgrounds do not clash in the finished film.

Color Wheel: A circular diagram of colors. The hue varies with the angle in the disc; saturation increases from the center outward. The entire disc is usually shown at the same intensity.

Comb Filter: An alternate (and better) method of performing Y/C separation. A comb filter is used in place of a chroma bandpass or chroma trap, providing better video quality. Named because the frequency response looks like a comb.

Comeback: A sarcastic or humorous response by one character to another.

Comedy Cones: Mechanisms of humor and gag techniques in a script.

Commercial Internet Exchange: See CIX.

Commercials: Jargon for television advertisements; usually one minute or less in length.

Common Gateway Interface (CGI): A programming language enabling one to use forms in a Website; a set of rules that describe how a Web server communicates with another piece of software on the same machine, and how the other piece of software (the "CGI program") talks to the Web server. Any piece of software can be a CGI program if it handles input and output according to the CGI standard. The computer graphics community also uses CGI as an abbreviation for Computer-generated Imagery.

Common Interchange Format: See CIF.

Compact Flash: A matchbook-sized memory card used in many digital cameras; capable of storing more than 200MB of information.

Compact Flash II: A new Compact Flash standard with increased capacity.

Complex Motion: Consists of several objects, or their parts, moving in a variety of directions, speeds and rhythms.

Complimentary Metal Oxide Semiconductor: See CMOS.

Component Video: A video signal that retains its original color information as separate elements and is technically superior to composite video. Betacam is an example of a component analog format; D1 is an example of a component digital format.

Composite: The result of layering two or more images to create one image. This can refer to various levels of still images that are layered over each other to create on image, or an entire animation that is layered over another to create on final animation. Compositing is considered a postproduction effects technique.

Composite Print: An additional print made after an approved answer print, incorporating the same corrections. Also known as Release Print.

Composite Video: A video signal in which the color (chrominance) and brightness (luminance) information has been combined into a single signal.

Compositing: The process of merging two or more images digitally to create one final image.

Compositor: A person whose job is to layer, overlay, or merge various images or scenes together to create one.

Compound: The flat, table like part of an animation stand the holds artwork while it is photographed.

Compression: A method of packing data in order to save disk storage space or download time. JPEGs are generally compressed graphics files. Compression is a technique to make a file or a data stream smaller for faster transmission, or to minimize storage space.

Compression File: A process for reducing file size, often called "zipping" or "archiving." The compressed file can contain one large file or several small files. The many-to-one compression makes file group identification, copying and transporting faster and easier.

Compression Mode: In reference to MusicMatch Jukebox, the process that determines the quality and format of the finished file.

Compression Ratio: A comparison between the size of an uncompressed data file divided by the size of the compressed version of that file, expressing the degree to which a compression algorithm can reduce file size as a ratio.

Compression, Lossless: Digitized video containing all original video information.

Compression, Lossy: Digitized video that, to save space, does not contain all original video information.

Compressor: See Codec.

Computer Animation: Takes advantages of the computer's ability to direct and generate a video image based on preprogrammed input. Key frame computer graphics that is interpolated by computer software to create motion or animation. Computer animation can be two-dimensional and designed to look like cel animation or three-dimensional like Disney Pixar's *Toy Story*.

Computer Graphic: All images that are created, manipulated, or generated by a computer.

Computer Technical Support: Maintains the computer systems in working order and develops custom software that may be required for special production requirements.

Computer Tomography: A method used to scan the human body to produce a computer-generated image.

Computer-Generated: Created on or by the computer. Can also describe any image that was not scanned from an existing original.

Computer-Generated Imagery (CGI): Often used to describe high-end computer graphic images and animation that have been incorporated into television commercials or Hollywood films. Any image created on the computer or that has been digitized can be referred to as Computer-Generated Imagery.

Computerized Animation Stand: A specialized animation stand that allows all camera movements to be preprogrammed and activated when the shutter is pressed, permitting greater accuracy and speed when filming.

Concatenated Transformations: A series of global transformations applied in sequence.

Concave: A property of a polygon that has at least one vertex bulge inward rather than outward.

concave

Concept: The term used to describe an idea for new media development.

Concept Art: Inspirational sketches or paintings used to establish the situations, color choices, or mood of a particular sequence, which were rendered in a wide range of media, from pastels and graphite, to watercolor and cut paper.

Concept Drawing: Drawings to work out the design, atmosphere, mood or other elements of a scene. See also Animation Drawing.

Concept Map: A browser, terms, definitions, or icons arranged in semantic proximity.

Consensual Reality: The world, or a simulation of a world, as viewed and comprehended by a society.

Conceptual Storyboard: To develop the basic visual ideas such as characters' actions, camera positions, timing of motions, and scene transitions.

Cone of Vision: The portion of the 3D environment that is seen through the camera. Also known as Pyramid of Vision.

Conference: An asynchronous online discussion area wherein a group of users may post information and comments.

Conform: Making the final edit according to a prepared scheme such as a rough cut or EDL. EDLs can be used to directly control conforming in an on-line edit suite (auto-conforming). Progressive versions of a project in the editing stage are known as conformations, often identified by date. Conformations are only of any significance on a large production where different editing departments should be sure to be working with the latest conformation.

Constraint: A rule of an inverse kinematics, or inverse dynamics, animation system that must be adhered to in solving the motion of all objects.

Context: A sensitive L-system; those whose performance is defined by the characteristics of the preceding module.

Contiguous: Related to data storage, this term describes a file whose elements are grouped together, not fragmented in separate locations on a disk.

Continuity: An uninterrupted, cohesive flow of one image to the other.

Continuous Branching: A feature of an interactive program that modifies the environment constantly in response to the user, rather than only at predetermined branching points or menus.

Continuous Masks: These have soft edges and different shades of gray.

Continuous Tone: An image containing gradient tones from white to black. Also known as Continuous Tone Image.

Contouring: The loss of detail when converting a gradient image to an image with a smaller number of colors.

Contrast: A term that describes lighting. High-contrast lighting shows a larger difference between light and dark, while low- or soft-contrast lighting brings out the midrange colors or values.

Control Panel: In a graphical user interface (GUI), a utility program that may be used to adjust parameters for system settings, such as volume, color and rate of response, to input devices.

Controlled Curves: See Spline.

Convergence: The degree to which all three electron beams of a color CRT meet at the same point on the screen. A poorly converged CRT will show the red, green, and blue components of the image slightly offset from each other, making the image look blurry and produces color fringes around the edges of objects.

Convex: A property of a polygon that bulges outward at all vertices.

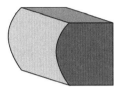

convex

Convolvotron: A system for controlling binaural sound production in VR.

Cookie: A message given to a Web browser by a Web server to identify Website users/visitors and possibly prepare customized pages for them. The most common meaning of "Cookie" on the Internet refers to a piece of information sent by a Web Server to a Web Browser that the Browser software is expected to save and to send back to the server whenever the browser makes additional requests from the server.

Cool: The experience of a feature containing unexpected utility or power.

Coordinates: The numbers that tell the engine where to position textures on mesh. The engine uses three texture coordinates, commonly called U (the width of the texture), V (the height), and W (used for depth if you are using a 3D procedural texture).

Coplanar: Two or more objects on the same 2D plane. If two pieces of paper are side-by-side flat on your desk, they're coplanar.

Copyright: The legal right to control how a song, lyric, program, book, or other piece of intellectual property is reproduced, distributed, and sold. Songs can have multiple copyrights: one for the author of the music, one for the author of the lyrics, and another for the musician or band performing the piece.

Coriolis Force: A force experienced by objects moving in rotating coordinate frames. Although we take Coriolis forces into account in our normal body motions, Coriolis forces in virtual environments (caused, for example, by centrifugal flight simulators) can lead to degradation in performance, and motion sickness. Similarly, pseudo-Coriolis forces caused by vection can also lead to motion sickness.

Courvoisier Cel: A common cel of the 30s and 40s, often trimmed to image, glued to background, and covered with a protective top cel.

Courvoisier Set Up: From 1937-46, Courvoisier Galleries, under commission from Walt Disney Productions, created unique backgrounds upon which to display production artwork. These backgrounds, or setups, are distinguished by their styling, matting, and official certificates and stamps of authenticity. Courvoisier Galleries were the first mass marketers of Disney animation artwork. Vintage Disney cels are often found on these types of setups. See also Re-Issue Courvoisier.

CPU (Central Processing Unit): A computer chip acting as the brain of the computer, controlling all other functions, and processing information fed to it by programs.

Cracking: A line(s) resembling tars, or cracks, in the paint.

Crane Shot: Implemented with a combination of boom, truck, and dolly movements.

Crane: A support mounting the camera over the compound.

Cray: The manufacturer of supercomputers. Cray Research, Inc.

CRC (Cyclic Redundancy Check): A data transmission error-checking procedure. It's a sending device that performs a complex calculation, generating a number based upon the data being transmitted, and sends that it to the receiving device, which performs the same calculation after transmission. If the results match, the transmission succeeds.

Creative: A standard term used for banner advertisements; can refer to the design or format of a banner, or to the process of creating a design.

Creative Team: Usually represented by the design studio, communications company, or advertising agency that developed the concept and the visual treatment.

Credits: Listings of all those involved in making a program, usually appearing at the end of a television program, film, or animation.

Creepy Crawlies: This term refers to a specific image artifact resulting from the NTSC system; when computer-generated text appears atop of the video clip being shown, along the edges of the box, or along the edges of the text, are some jaggies "rolling" up (or down) the picture—these are the creepy-crawlies. Also known as Zipper.

CRM: See Customer Relationship Management.

Crop Area: The area of the image that will be captured by an image manipulation tool, usually marked by a colored or blinking box. The crop area can be changed by adjusting the size and placement of this box.

Crop Marks: Short, fine lines placed around the edges of a page to designate where the paper is to be trimmed while at the print shop.

Crop Tool: A editing process for selecting an area of an image or photograph.

Cross Color: This occurs when the video decoder incorrectly interprets high-frequency luma information (brightness) to be chroma information (color), resulting in color being displayed where it should not.

Cross Section Extrusion: A technique of skinning.

Cross-Platform: Files usable/executable with different operating systems. For example, Virtus WalkThrough, a 3D animator program, can produce "cross-compatible" animation files for Macintosh and DOS/Windows machines; "power" Macs allow one to change to the PC work-mode; "power" PCs can handle Mac software/files.

Crosstalk: An undesirable sound that bleeds into a connection or isolated audio track from an adjacent tape track.

CRT: See Cathode Ray Tube.

CSS: See Cascading Style Sheet.

Cubes: These are usually modeled as six-sided, closed, 3D objects.

Cubic Environment Map: A mapping space comprised of six textures applied to the various faces of a virtual cube.

Cubical Projection: A variation of the flat projection method; repairs the map on each of the six sides of a cube.

Culling: The process of removing invisible pieces of geometry, sending only potentially visible geometry to the graphics subsystem; it involves rejecting objects not in the view frustum.

Cursor: A small blinking character on the computer screen indicating where the next typed character will appear; often controlled by a mouse. Also known as Pointer.

Curved Interpolation: The technique used to calculate frames more sophisticated than linear interpolation.

Custom Background: See Presentation Background.

Custom Filters: A tool used to alter the pixels of a digital image. Filters are commonly used in paint programs to perform such functions as emboss, wave, blur, and distort.

Custom/Hand Prepared Background: A background created by an artist for the purpose of enhancing a cel.

Customer Relationship Management (CRM): A term used to describe the sophisticated personalization tools developed by vendors to help define customer groups and target them with the right products and services. Companies use Web-based CRM products to help learn who their most profitable customers are on the Web, and how to target them more effectively.

CUT: A direct transition from one scene to the next; the removal of unwanted film footage; an individual piece of music. See also Track.

Cut-Copy-Paste: A technique used to duplicate objects.

Cutouts: An animation technique in which small, flat, joined figures, usually made of heavy paper, are placed over a background, manipulated under the camera then photographed.

Cutout/Trimmed Cels: The images on cels were often cut out of the full sheet to make them fit into scrapbooks or small frames; they were also carefully trimmed to the outlines of the character so the cel could be applied to a background with other cels without having to worry about where the edges of the cel would fall within the image; generally worth less than images on full sheets.

Cutouts on Cels: An animation technique combining cel and cuts methods. The cutout figures are pasted onto cells, placed over a background then photographed.

Cutting Room: The editor's work area.

Cyberculture: A collection of cultures and cultural products, with background stories, exist on, and/or are made possible by the Internet.

Cyberdeck: The machinery used to create and maintain cyberspace.

Cyberia: A pun on Siberia. Also an AutoDesk.

Cybernaut: A voyager in virtual reality.

Cybernetic Simulation: A dynamic model of a world filled with objects exhibiting lesser or greater degrees of intelligence.

Cybernetics: The study of communication and control processes; often used to indicate a conceptual connection to, or control by, computers.

Cyberpunk: Originally a cultural sub-genre of science fiction taking place in a not-so-distant, over-industrialized society. Named for the work of William Gibson and Bruce Sterling, it has evolved into a cultural label encompassing many different types of humans, machines and punk attitudes, as well as clothing and lifestyle choices.

Cyberscope: A viewer attached to a monitor enabling stereoscopic viewing of software. Also a term used to describe controlled images.

Cyberspace Playhouse: A social place where people play roles in simulations.

Cyberspace: The "electronic" world as perceived on a computer screen. The term is often used in opposition to the "real" world.

Cycle: A series of drawings photographed repeatedly. The last drawing moves logically into the first, to create the appearance of continuous, repetitive motion.

Cyclic Redundancy Check: See CRC.

Cylinders/Cones: Polygonal objects shaped by the following variables: radius, height, number of longitudinal divisions, number of latitudinal divisions, and whether they are "capped" or not.

Cylindrical Projection: Projection that applies maps to surface faces by wrapping the sides of the map around the shape until the two ends meet behind the object.

D

D1: D2: D3: Digital video recording and playback formats. The D1 system uses component video while the D2 and D3 systems use composite video. By using fully digitized video in recording and playback, many problems such as generation loss and distortion are minimized or eliminated. The digital formats use mainly a 19mm wide magnetic tape (3/4").

DAC: See Digital-to-Analog Converter.

Dailies: A print of the previous day's shooting, used to check the results for correctness. They are used mainly in feature production. Also known as Rushes.

Dark Map: The texture used to blend with the base map to create a new, darker texture.

DAT: See Digital Audio Tape.

Data: Any type of information stored in a computer; all data must be in a digital form.

Data File: A list of numbers that define models in a way that can be understood by computer programs.

Data Processing: The manipulation of data by a computer.

Data Projector: A device that projects output from a computer onto a remote screen; older data projectors are large and heavy, and use tubes to create the image; newer units weigh less than 20lb and combine an internal LCD (Liquid Crystal Display) panel with a light source; generally accept SVGA output and often standard VCR/TV video.

Data Rate: The amount of information per second used to represent a movie, often expressed in KBps (KiloBytes/sec).

A single-speed CD-ROM movie is usually made at a data rate of 100 KBps, and a double-speed CD-ROM movie at about 200 KBps. The data rate of uncompressed NTSC video is about 27 MBps (MegaBytes/sec).

Data Rate Spikes: Short sections of a movie that have significantly higher data rates than the rest of the movie. If not properly managed, spikes may cause dropped frames or other problems.

Database: A structured set of records, such as a mailing list; a Web browser can access a public database via Perl scripts. When data is structured as a table in a single file, users need only browse the page and use the browser's "Find" feature. To search a relational database using many files a sophisticated CGI script is required to access data.

DataGlove: A glove wired with sensors connected to a computer system for gesture recognition; used for tactile feedback and often enables navigation through a virtual environment and interaction with 3D objects within.

DataSpace: A visualized representation of complex information.

DataSuit: Similar to a DataGlove, but designed for the entire body.

Date Rate Limiting: The ability of a program or codec to control the size of the final compressed movie to meet specified data rates.

DCS (Desktop Color Separation): A file format that creates four-color separations.

DCS 2.0: A Desktop Color Separation file format used to save a CMYK image for color separation, with the option of saving spot color and alpha channels, and an optional low resolution file to preview and laser print.

DCT (Discrete Cosine Transform): An invertible, discrete, orthogonal transformation. A mathematical process used in MPEG video encoding to transform blocks of pixel values into blocks of spatial frequency values with lower-frequency components organized into the upper-left corner, allowing the high-frequency components in the lower-right corner to be discounted or discarded.

DDE (Dynamic Data Exchange): A Windows' method of supporting the exchange of commands and data between two applications.

DDL (Dynamic Link Library): A Windows' code module loaded and linked at runtime then unloaded when finished executing.

Dead Air: This term refers to a lack of dialog or action in the script. The animation director must hold on a reaction of a character to fill time.

Debug: To isolate and correct errors/malfunctions in computer software or hardware

Decimation: This term refers to when a video signal is digitized so that 100 samples are produced, but only every other one is stored or used, the signal is decimated by a factor of 2:1. The image is now _ of its original size, since _ of the data is missing; a quick-and-easy method used for image scaling.

Deck: A physical space containing an array of instruments, which enable a player to act within, and feel a part of, a virtual space.

Decode: In multimedia, this term refers to decompressing a compressed (encoded) file so that it may be displayed. Codecs do this decoding while the video/audio is played.

Decoder: A program that converts MP3 files back into WAV files.

Dedicated Line: An ongoing connection to the Internet using an individual phone line.

Deep Space Blocking: A type of blocking associated with single-camera productions, particularly those shot on location. The depth of the "set" is emphasized by the ability of one actor to be positioned near the camera and another far away; the actors may move toward one another, or participate in independent actions.

Default Setting: Typically used in computer programs to set variables or values to a common setting.

Default: The standard setting of an optional parameter.

Defense Simulation Internet (DSI): An Internet component that supports DIS and SIMNET, and permits scheduled guaranteed bandwidth.

Deformation: To change the shape of an object using a controlling force.

Deformation Parameters: Setting that allow an animator to control the various properties by bending skin, and to manipulate single or groups of vertices on the skin's surface.

Deformation With Splines and Patches: Using a Spline or patch as the agent to deform the object that is associated with them.

Defragment: To place all data on a hard disk in contiguous sectors, avoiding gaps between parts of a file(s) spread geographically on the disk.

Degree: High exponent in the mathematical formulas that generate curves.

Degrees of Freedom: Used to express the ability of a joint to rotate around and/or to translate along one or several axes.

Deinterlace: To remove the interlacing artifacts caused by the two-fields-per-frame nature of video.

Delta Frames: Frames containing only the changes from the previous frame, created by codecs, which use temporal compression. Also known as Difference Frames.

Density: Related to computing, the degree to which data is spatially distributed on a storage medium.

Depth Cueing: In 3D graphics creation, it is a process resulting in the illusion that objects fade into the distance.

Depth of Field: The area in front of, and behind the subject within focus.

Dequantization: The reverse process of quantization.

De-Rez: Techniques used to make pixels less visible in a display.

Derivative Product: Work that adapts material from a previous creation.

Design: The look, feel, and structure of a Website. The synergy and synthesis of three aspects: sensory, conceptual, and reactive.

Desktop Color Separation: See DCS.

Despeckle Filter: Filter that removes any specs from the image and blurs the entire image except for any edges.

Development of the Character: Development that includes both drawing and building models.

Device Independent Bitmap: See DIB.

Device Independent Color: See DIC.

DFX: See Drawing Interchange Format.

DHTML (Dynamic Hypertext Mark-up Language): An HTML extension that allows Web pages to react to the end users' input, such as displaying a Web page based on the type of browser or computer end users are using to view.

Dial Numbers: The camera operator can determine whether a given exposure has been shot by comparing the dial numbers on his camera stand against those on the exposure sheet.

Dialog: Speech—the portion of the soundtrack that is recorded by the voice artists and spoken by the characters on the screen. Also known as Dialogue.

Dialog Block: The lines of dialog that make up a character's speech block.

Dialog Box: Any type of screen in a graphical user interface that displays or requests information from the user. See also GUI.

Dialog Devices: Writers' tools used to jazz up dialog, making it more interesting.

Dial-Up: Any line or connection that can be addressed by a modem and is established by a switched-circuit connection using the telephone system.

DIB (Device Independent Bitmap): A Windows graphics file format.

DIC (Device Independent Color): A color model that can be transported between platforms with no alteration to the color information.

Dichotic Filter: A special optical filter that reflects certain light wavelengths while allowing others to pass through.

Differential Gain: This term refers to the color saturation changes when luma levels change (it isn't supposed to); for a video system, the better the differential gain—that is, the smaller the number specified—the better the system will determine the correct color.

Diffuse Color: An object's surface property defined in the Phong lighting model. An object's diffuse color is reflected equally in all directions. Visually, it is flat or dull color.

Diffuse Interreflection: Calculated by the rendering technique of radiosity.

Diffuse Light: A type of light that originates from a specific source, but scatters in all directions.

Diffuse Reflection: The light reflected from an object equally in each direction.

Diffusion Dithering: A method of dithering that randomly distributes pixels rather than using a set pattern.

Digital: A form of representation in which information or objects (digits) are broken down into separate pieces. For example, numbers.

Digital/Digitalization/Digitized: The process of converting video or audio signals, normally in waveform, into 1s and 0s (binary), which can be processed by a computer.

Digital 8: Compresses video using standard DV compression, yet records it allowing the use of standard Hi-8 tapes, which results in a DV "box" that can also play standard Hi-8 and 8mm tapes.

Digital Art: Art in which information is translated for use by computer.

Digital Audio Tape (DAT): A standard medium and technology for the digital recording of audio on tape at a professional level of quality.

Digital Audio: Sound or music that is stored as a series of bits rather that by a continuously varying (analog) signal.

Digital Compositing: The art of combining video frames as digital, rather than as analog signals.

Digital Flipbook: A sequence of image files displayed in the area of the screen, ranging from small to the full screen.

Digital Ink & Paint System (DIPS): A computer-based systems used for 2D cartoons to replace time-consuming manual inking and painting with faster, more flexible digital tools.

Digital Light Projector (DLP): Unlike a film projector, its technology does not involve the use of a shutter because there is no film being mechanically pulled through a gate, there is no need to douse the light; the screen luminance output of approximately 12.5 ft is roughly equivalent to the current SMPTE standard for nominal screen luminance; the mirrors tilt on and off to control the amount of light reflected onto a screen unlike any frame-based system.

Digital Media: Works, including film, in which information is translated for use by computer.

Digital Modem: A special type of modem that connects a computer to a separate phone line for DSL service.

Digital Painting: Creating artwork directly on a computer as opposed to using traditional media and scanning the artwork.

Digital Postproduction: The part of the production team responsible for scanning, retouching, and compositing all layers of visual effects, computer animation, and live action.

Digital Print Order Feature (DPOF): Allows pictures to be selected in the camera for future direct-from-memory-card printing on photo-finishing machines equipped with this feature.

Digital Ripper: A device that extracts CD tracks then converts them into WAV files on you computer's hard disk. See also Ripping.

Digital Service: A term that refers to what a telephone company calls a telecommunications line for data transmission that has rates of data transfer specified at predetermined levels. See also DSL Service (Digital Subscriber Line).

Digital Signal: A method of representing information using 1s and 0s (binary), which is interpreted by a computer; they are easy to manipulate and are not degraded when copied, modified, or transmitted.

Digital Signal Processor (DSP): A separate processor, built into some sound cards that offloads/relieves audio processing from the computer's CPU.

Digital Subscriber Line (DSL): A direct 24-hour link to the Internet at speeds of at least 144K, six times the speed of the average modem. See also Digital Service.

Digital-to-Analog Converter (DAC): The sound card component that plays sounds stored in a file.

Digital VCR: A device similar to analog VCRs in that tape is used for storage; rather than recording an analog audio/video signal, digital VCRs record digital signals, usually using compressed audio/video.

Digital Versatile Disc: See DVD.

Digital Video Effects: See DVE.

Digital Watermark: A pattern of bits inserted into a digital image, audio, or video file that identifies the file's copyright information; named for the faintly visible watermarks imprinted on stationery to identify the manufacturer; the purpose is to provide copyright protection for intellectual property in digital format.

Digital Zoom: An electronic enlargement of part of the image, simulating an optical zoom lens at a telephoto setting; the image is actually cropped resulting in loss of surrounding pixels and decreased resolution; in some digicams, interpolation is used to offset this loss. See Interpolation.

Digitizing Tablet: A pen-based input system, resembling a sketch pad. Pressure of the pen on the tablet is translated in electronic dot patterns, often used by delivery companies to record signatures upon package receipt.

Dimensions: The width, height, and depth of a 3D object.

DIPS: See Digital Ink & Paint System.

Direct Evaluation: The process of determining the apparent color of an object at a particular point by direct evaluation of the lighting model, as opposed to interpolating from previously determined values.

Direct Manipulation: A term coined by Shneiderman to reflect the use of computer icons or text as if they were real objects.

Direct Memory Access (DMA): A capability provided by some computer bus architectures that allows data to be sent directly from an attached device (such as a disk drive) to the memory on the computer's motherboard—the microprocessor is freed from involvement with the data transfer, thus speeding up overall computer operation.

Direct Numerical Description: The process by which 3D objects can be modeled by typing the numbers that describe the object directly.

Directional Light: A light source that shines from the same direction at every point in the scene; used as a shortcut for modeling distant light sources.

Directory: A term commonly mistaken for a search engine. For example, Yahoo is a directory. A directory does not make use of a spider or robot, and is usually divided into categories.

Directory Service: Networking software with the capacity to provide information about resources available on the network, including files, printers, data sources, applications, or other users.

DIS: See Distributed Interactive Simulations.

Disc: A thin, round platter used to store various types of information in analog or digital formats as in a Compact Disc.

Discrete Access: In network technology, an access method requiring each workstation to have a separate connection to the host.

Discrete Cosine Transform: See DCT.

Disk: A circular, enclosed magnetic storage medium on which information may be accessed randomly, as opposed to sequentially.

Disney Seal: Full cels laminated and embossed with "original hand-painted movie film cel." Larger than the seals used today, they were primarily sold in the 1970s.

Disneyland Art Corner: Common cels of the mid-1950s to the early '70s. They were trimmed, against a litho background, and had a gold seal attached to the back.

Disorientation: The confusion about navigational distances and directions.

Displacement Maps: A filter used to alter both the orientation and 3D position of the surface. These shift pixels and distort an image according to luminance values of one image to affect the target image.

Dissolve: A camera effect in which one scene gradually fades out as another simultaneously fades in to replace it; commonly used as scene transitions in animation. This term can also mean to fade two adjacent scenes together, overlapping images.

Distance Education/Learning: Instruction that takes place when the student and instructor are separated by physical space and/or time; For example, correspondence courses; networked computers, especially those linked into the Internet, provide many remote education opportunities.

Distortion Morphing: A method of morphing that distorts a single image or sequence without fading into another.

Distributed Interactive Simulations (DIS): Based on SIMNET.

Distributed Rendering: A method of sending portions of a rendering job to different computers on a network.

Dither Pattern: The particular pattern of threshold values used in dithering; some dither patterns are random, while others are applied as repeated tiles across entire image.

Dithered: Needed to display a full-color graphic image on a 256-color monitor by simulate the colors it cannot display. This involves combining pixels from a 256-color palette into patterns that approximate other colors. At a distance, the human eye merges the pixels into a single color, while up close, the graphic image will appear pixelated and speckled.

Dithering: The blending colors to modify colors or produce new ones. See Dithered.

DLL (Dynamic Link Library): A collection of small programs, any of which can be called upon when needed by a larger program running in the computer; often given a ".dll" file name suffix.

DLP: See Digital Light Projector.

DMA: See Direct Memory Access.

DNS (Domain Name System): Translates URL text addresses (i.e.: grantasticdesigns.com) into a numeric Internet address (i.e.: 201.214.12.6).

Dodecahedron: A 12-sided rectangular polyhedral.

Dodging: A process that lightens a specific area of an image.

Dolly: A transition of the camera along horizontal (X) axis.

Domain Name: A multi-part name usually consisting of a host server name ("www"), the organization or entity's name ("animationcareers"), and the purpose of the organization ("com" meaning "commercial"), used to locate a particular Website. Also the unique name that identifies an Internet site.

Domain Name System: See DNS.

Dot: This term refers to the printing image. The screen dots produced by a printer to make an image on paper. The screen is also referred to as a halftone, which is the only way to print shades of colors.

Dot Gain: The undesirable spreading and enlarging of ink dots on paper, which causes colors or shades to look darker.

Dot Pitch: A measure of closeness between the phosphor triads on the face of a color CRT; triads are arranged in a hexagonal pattern, and the dot pitch is the distance from the center of one triad to the center of any of its six neighbors, usually specified in millimeters (mm).

Dots Per Inch (DPI): A resolution for scanning and printing devices.

Double Buffering: The creation of a back-buffer and off-screen buffer to hold accumulating pixels.

Downsample: The process of reducing the sample rate of a digital sound to reduce file size. See also Subsampling.

Downward Compatibility: This exists when files created with new software upgrades are compatible with earlier versions of the software.

DPI: See Dots Per Inch.

DPOF: See Digital Print Order Feature.

DRAM: See Dynamic Random Access Memory.

Draw Order: The back-to-front order of polygons drawing atop one another with the last appearing to be in front.

Draw Rate: See Frames Per Second.

Drawing Interchange Format (DXF): A universal file format.

Drawing Program: A program that produces graphical objects rather than bitmaps, which are created by paint programs.

Drawings: The beginning artwork prior to the painting of a cel. An animator must draw 24 individual drawings to create one second of film. These consist of rough drawings, done by key animators, to establish pose and action, and clean up drawings or retracings, done by clean-up artists, to produce finished art ready to be transferred to a cel.

Drawn-On-Film: An animation technique in which the image is drawn, painted, or scratched directly on the film stock.

Drawn-On-Paper: An animation technique in which the animator's drawings are photographed rather than transferred to cels.

Dreaming: The state of mind during sleep wherein vivid colored imagery becomes realistic—a natural counterpart to virtual reality.

Droid: A puppet that embodies a human intellect (as in android).

Drop Frame/Non-Drop Frame: NTSC's method of handling color information—color video needs to run at 29.97fps rather than video's typical 30fps, and as a result, non-drop frame time code adds 3.5 seconds per hour. Videotapes are "black-encoded" with either drop or non-drop frame time code prior to an edit session.

Drop Shadow: A drop shadow gives image depth by creating a shaded offset behind a selected image.

Drop-Down Menu: A term often used in an online form. For example, Pull-down Menu.

Drum Scanners: Professional-quality scanners where original transparencies are positioned on a drum. The drum then rotates at high speeds then a photo multiplier directs light.

Dry Brush: A painting technique in which the brush is dipped in paint, brushed on a surface to remove most of the paint, then used to create brush strokes with a rough, grainy, irregular look.

DS-1: 1.544 megabits per second.

DSI: See Defense Simulation Internet.

DSL Service: A direct 24-hour link to the Internet at speeds of at least 144K, six times the speed of the average modem. See also Digital Service.

DSL: See Digital Subscriber Line.

DSP: See Digital Signal Processor.

DTV: Digital TV or Desk Top Video.

Dub: The process of copying one tape to another. Also a term used to describe an audio or videotape duplicate.

Duotone: The application of two colors to provide richer tones than a monotone (single-color image, usually grayscale) can provide. A good duotone image can simulate a wider range of the color spectrum than two colors used separately. Duotones also use a hue (color) to set the mood for a photo in a more stunning way than a full-color image can.

Duplicating: An independent copy of an object.

DV: This term refers to a specific Digital Video standard, an electrical standard used to transfer data from digital video cameras to computers and other digital video devices; resolution is 720x480 at a frame rate of 29.97 (North American—NTSC—standard) and a data rate of 3.6 MB per second. Also known as IEEE 1394.

DVD (Digital Versatile Disc): A CD format capable of supplanting CD-R and CD-RW.

DVD-ROM: The version of the DVD disc format designed for computers similar to a fast (8x), large (4.7: 17 GB) CD-ROM. It can hold any type of computer data and does not require MPEG.

DVD-Video: A version of the DVD disc format used for storage of prerecorded movies, capable of replacing VHS; the DVD-Video specification uses MPEG.

DVE (Digital Video Effects): A term that refers to a device used to manipulate video images.

DVNR: See Digital Video Noise Reduction.

Dye Sublimation: A continuous-tone printing process in which a solid printing medium is converted into a gas before it hits paper. A method of photographic quality color printing .

Dye Transfer: High-quality photographic reproductions of key scenes from Disney movies, prepared for many years as gifts for special studio guests.

Dynamic Data Exchange: See DDE.

Dynamic HTML: HTML instructions (Hyper-Text Markup Language) that enable Web pages to react to user input and produce content that changes each time it is viewed. With this coding, Web pages are created "on the fly," as the information is delivered to your desktop; technologies for producing dynamic HTML include CGI scripts, Server-Side Includes (SSI), Cookies, Java, JavaScript, Cold Fusion, and ActiveX. Also known as DHTML.

Dynamic Hypertext Mark-up Language: See DHTML.

Dynamic Lighting: The changes in lighting effects on objects as they and the observer move.

Dynamic Link Library: See DDL.

Dynamic Random Access Memory (DRAM): A common type of random access memory (RAM) for personal computers and workstations; dynamic in that, unlike static RAM (SRAM), it needs to have its storage cells refreshed or given a new electronic charge every few milliseconds; DRAM stores each bit in a storage cell consisting of a capacitor and a transistor.

Dynamics: The way that objects interact and move; the rules that govern all actions and behaviors within the environment.

Dynamic Simulation: Real-world phenomena (such as friction) is imitated by using dynamic simulation. Achieved by attaching physical properties (such as mass) to objects then manipulating forces that produce motion in objects over time. It calculates the motion of objects through time by providing the software with some of the physical properties of an object.

Dynamic SQL: Modifies queries based on user data, environment variables, and previously returned query results. Can also increase processing efficiency by executing multiple queries and sending them to multiple databases from a single browser request.

Dynamic Web Page: Web pages that respond to users' requests and gather information from them; often contain built-in links to a relational database, from which they extract data based on input from the user (using dynamic SQL), and contain very little text.

E

Ease Function: Interpolation controls that allow for the adjustment of an animation in between key frames. Such functions include ease-in and ease-out.

Ease In: The increase in speed, or easing into speed. Also known as Slow In.

Ease Out: A decrease in speed, or easing out speed. Also known as Show Out.

Eccentricity: An attribute of the Blinn shading model that controls highlight size.

E-Commerce: The buying and selling of services or commodities via the Internet, often using instant electronic payment. Electronic Commerce.

Edge: A term defined by two adjacent surfaces.

Edge Blanking: The black part of the video signal that falls outside the area displayed on a TV screen; most capture cards include some amount of edge blanking around the captured image. Commonly referred to as Edge Noise or Overscan.

Edge Coding: The time code printed on the edge of film, giving a set number to each frame.

Edit Controller: A complex system that controls the actions of video and audio recording or playback machines.

Edit Decision List: See EDL.

Editing: The process of changing or manipulating data to arrange various shots, scenes and sequences, or the elements of the soundtrack, in the order desired to create the finished film.

Editor: A person who deletes or adds scenes to a picture by following the instructions of the director, and who keeps the soundtracks in sync.

EDL (Edit Decision List): The file or list of edits (in-and-out points, reel numbers, and edit types) prepared during the offline edit and completed in the online edit resulting in an assembled master.

Edutainment: Entertaining and educational digital media products.

Effector: The endpoint of an inverse kinematic chain translated to pose the rest of the chain.

Effects Animation: The animation of non-character movements, such as rain, smoke, lightning, or water.

Egocenter: The sense of personal viewpoints that determine one's location in virtual reality. See also Projection Point.

E-IDE (Enhanced Integrated Drive Electronics):
Extensions to the IDE standard providing faster data transfer and allowing access to larger drives, including CD-ROM and tape drives, using ATAPI. E-IDE was adopted as a standard by ANSI in 1994. ANSI calls it Advanced Technology Attachment-2 (ATA-2) or Fast ATA.

Elapsed Time: Absolute timing values.

Electromagnetic Forces (EMF): A term that describes effects on human tissues that are poorly understood and that may constitute an important hazard for tracking and display devices.

Electronic Art: Art requiring electric devices.

Electronic Magazine: A name given to a Website that is either (a) modeled after a print magazine or a magazine that is only available online or via e-mail.

Electronic Poetry: Time-based poetry that may include interactive and generative elements.

Electronic Publishing: The creation and distribution of computer-generated media.

E-Mail: A system used to transmit messages digitally via a communications network, the online communications between computer users, and the most frequently used communications tool on the Internet. Electronic Mail allows communication with one or thousands of users in less time and for less money than conventional communication services.

Embed Tag: HTML code that specifies how a graphic or movie will be included within a Web page.

Emboss: Adds dimension to a graphic image by making the image appear carved as a projection from a flat background.

EMF: See Electromagnetic Forces.

Emissive Color: An object surface property sometimes used with the Phong lighting model; an object's emissive color is independent of any illumination, therefore appearing as if the object were emitting the color.

Emitter: A geometric entity that creates particles.

Emotion: Helps to define the mood of the story.

Encapsulation PostScript (EPS): A graphics file format that can store both raster and vector graphics.

Encode: In multimedia, this term means to compress a file. See also Compression.

Encoder: A program that converts WAV files to MP3 files by saving only the audible sounds and throwing away the rest.

Encryption: The process of converting information into undecipherable codes; invented by Phil PGP Zimmermann.

Endoscopic: The part of a family of new surgical procedures that avoid cutting major portions of the patient in favor of making small holes through which tools and sensors are inserted and the surgery performed. In a VR or tele-presence application, the surgeon manipulates the tools by observing the surgery site on a monitor via optical fibers and a tiny video camera.

Engine: The underlying software that drives a particular new media product.

Enhanced Integrated Device Electronics (EIDE): A format used by disk drives, CD-ROMs, and other data storage devices to communicate; handles more data channels than the standard IDE.

Environment: A computer-generated model that can be experienced from the "inside" as if it were a location.

Environmental Maps: This reflects objects surrounding the mapped object as well as the environment surrounding the reflective surfaces.

Environmentally Sensitive L-system: Those systems defined by environmental characteristics such as exposure to light and collision with objects.

Epistemology: The philosophical study of learning and the acquisition of knowledge.

EPS (Encapsulated PostScript): A graphics file format; can store both raster and vector graphics.

Equalization: A term that describes the adjustment of relative output of frequencies in a given range to provide a more balanced sound.

Equalizer: A hardware or software device allowing one to filter specific frequency ranges. It equalizes the audio output to speakers.

Establishing Shot: A shot, normally taken from a great distance or from a "bird's eye view," that establishes where the action is about to occur.

Ethernet: A common local area network (LAN) specification used for data communication. The IEEE 802.3 standard.

EtherTalk: Ethernet protocol used by Apple computers.

Evolutionary Art: Animation based on simulated living systems and artificial intelligence principles.

Exaggerated Gestures: Gestures often used to punctuate dramatic deliveries.

Exchange: In telecommunications, a coordination point established by a common carrier in a geographical area wherein the central office support and the equipment for communications services are provided.

Exchangeable Image File (EXIF): The JPEG compression mode used by most digicams.

Executable Program: A type of computer program, typically found in DOS with the extension .exe that performs a function or carries out a series of commands.

EXIF: See Exchangeable Image File.

Exoskeletal Devices: Rigid external supports to gloves and arm motion systems to provide force feedback.

Expansion Slot: A socket on a microcomputer motherboard into which an expansion board may be inserted.

Export: To save a file in a different format (that of another program). For example, many Adobe Photoshop files are exported to become GIF or JPEG files.

Exposition: Information needed by the audience to understand the story or a character's motivations.

Exposure: The subjection of a piece of film to light producing a latent image on emulsion.

Exposure Compensation: A feature on most digicams that allows manual override of the camera's light meter to achieve better exposure under difficult lighting conditions.

Exposure Sheet: The frame-by-frame instructions for a camera operator that accompany the artwork sent to be photographed.

EXT: A term meaning Exterior that describes the location in the slugline, and is always abbreviated in capital letters.

Extensible Hypertext Mark-up Language: See XHTML.

Extension: A small program that plugs into a larger one and provides increased functionality; the letters that appear after the dot (.) in the name of an MS-DOS file to classify the file type.

External Flash Synch: Allows connection to other flash units instead of (or in addition to) the digicam's built-in flash; very useful for experimenting with off-camera lighting effects and for use with studio strobes.

Extract: To decode a file encoded for network transmission, usually with reference to the uuencode/uudecode UNIX utility.

Extrapolation: A change of state of an object over time before or after the previously defined key frames, used to cycle animation. For example, to animate walking, just key frame the legs for a single step and cycle the rest.

Extreme: An animator's drawing that shows the outside limits, or "extremes," of movement that a character will experience.

Extreme Long Shot: A camera shot that presents environments seen from very far away.

Eye Dropper Tool: An image-editing tool used to select a color from the current image.

Eye Tracking: Devices that measure direction of gaze. Most HMDs do not currently support eye tracking directly.

Eyeball in the Hand: A metaphor used for visualized tracking wherein the handheld tracker is connected to motion of the projection point of the display.

EyeGen: An HMD made by virtual research that combines visual and auditory display.

F

Face: a collection of three or more vertexes tied together to form a small triangular surface. Most 3D programs use three-sided faces, but some support four-sided as well. A collection of faces is referred to as a 'mesh.' Each face also has a special entity tied to it called a "normal." The normal defines which side of the face is considered to be the inside of an object, and which is the outside.

Facet Shading: A method of shading wherein the shading normal vector is taken from the geometric normal of the surface actually drawn, making the surface patches visible, especially if they are planar.

Facets: Planar surfaces that define most 3D objects.

Facsimile: A digital document or scanned image transmitted to another fax machine or computer using telephone lines; a form of e-mail. Also known as Fax.

Fade: An optical effect in which the screen gradually brightens as a shot appears (fade in) or gradually darkens as a shot goes to black or another blank color (fade out). Sound also fades in or out when the soundtrack gradually changes from silence to sound, or vice versa.

1 fade in, 2 fade out

Fade In: Increasing an audio or video from no signal to maximum signal. Often follows a fade out to indicate major divisions within a production. Also the first words typed in a script. Literally means "to begin."

Fade Out: Decreasing an audio or video from maximum signal to zero. Often indicates the end of a segment. Also the last words in a script which means "the end."

Falling Rocks: The obstacles hurled at the driver during the story.

Fall-off: The point where the light hits the object. A fast fall-off happens when there is a single bright light source hitting a subject causing a dramatic image with bright highlights and dark shadowed areas. A Slow fall-off occurs when there are multiple light sources or hazy lighting conditions, resulting in a slow fall-off from light to dark.

Far Clipping Plane: A term that defines the most distant area that can be seen by the camera. Also known as Yon Plane.

Fast Start: A Fast Start movie contains the data needed to view in QuickTime—it is stored at the beginning of the file.

FDDI (Fiber Distributed Data Interface): A set of ANSI and ISO standards for data transmission on fiber optic lines in a LAN that can extend in range up to 200 km (124 miles).

Feather: To softly fade a piece of sound. A graphics tool used to soften the edges of an image.

Feathering: The process of gradually dissipating an image's edge making it appear blurry.

Feature: A full-length animated film, usually 60 to 120 minutes in length.

Ferroelectric Liquid Crystals (FLC): An animation or moving picture file format originally created by Animator Pro, FLC files contain one or more frames, enabling one to view animated pictures from the screen when files are displayed. An "FLC" file has the extension ".flc."

Fiber Distributed Date Interface: See FDDI.

Field: The area to be photographed, and usually the area in which the animator draws.

Field Guide: A punched sheet of heavy acetate, printed to indicate the sizes of all standard fields, which, when placed over the artwork, indicate the area in which the action will take place. Graphs with concentric rectangles can be used to specify the exact position of text and graphics within the frame. Grids of concentric rectangles are used to position the still elements and the action within the frame.

Field of View (FOV): The angle in degrees of the visual field. Most HMDs offer 60 to 90 degrees FOV. Because our two eyes have overlapping 140 degree FOV, binocular or total FOV is roughly 180 degrees horizontal by 120 degrees vertical. A feeling of immersion seems to arise with FOV greater than 60 degrees. See also Geometric FOV.

Fielding: This term refers to the size of the area on the artwork that falls within the sight of the camera. For example, a 12 field is roughly 12 inches across, and a 9 field is 9 inches across.

FIF (Fractal Image Format): A method of storing raster graphics and compressing them with fractal transform formulas.

File: A collection of data organized on storage media, such as a hard disk or floppy diskette.

File Format: The specific type of organization used by a file. It contains descriptions of object geometry exclusive to specific computer programs and is not portable.

File Server: In a computer network, the central computer that controls network functions.

Fill Tool: A common paining tool used to fill a solid area with color.

File Transfer Protocol (FTP): The common procedure used for downloading and uploading files over the Internet.

Fill Rate: The number of pixels rendered (textured and shaded) over time (millions of pixels per second, MPPS).

Filler Objects: Often of spherical shape, these objects are positioned at the joints that have wide rotation angles.

Fillets: These allow the creation of a custom trim that extends along the edge of an image.

Fill-in Light: Ambient light.

Filtering: A method used to determine the color of a pixel based on texture maps. A close-up view of a polygon reveals that the texture map does not have enough information to determine the real color of each pixel on the screen, so through interpolation (a technique of using information of the real pixels surrounding the unknown pixel to determine its color based on mathematical averages) the correct pixel is calculated.

Finished Drawing: This term refers to the line quality of a drawing.

Finite Element Modeling: Decomposition of complex structures into small, simple elements to manage engineering computations.

Firewall: Used on a local area network (LAN), connected to a larger network, as the security systems that prevent outside intrusion as well as inside information from getting out.

FireWire: A data transfer standard IEEE 1394, which allows video, audio and other digital information to move between peripheral devices such as DV cameras.

Fitting: Removes small gaps between surfaces.

Fixed Focus: The camera's focus is preset to a distance at which most subjects or objects will be in focus from near to far. Not as precise as autofocus.

Fixed Repetition: An instructional design feature that repeats a lesson or module in the same way.

Flag: A shadow-casting device made of cloth stretched over a metal frame. Distinct types of flags include the cutter, finger, target, and teaser.

Flash: Vector graphic animation software from Macromedia that allows Flash graphics to appear the same in all browsers, as long as the plug-in is installed.

Flashback: A scene that flashes back in time. Also a technique used to give exposition.

Flashpath: A floppy-disk-sized shell into which a SmartMedia memory card is inserted so that images may be transferred directly to the computer through its floppy drive. Despite its convenience, it requires batteries and is slower than a PC (memory) card reader.

Flat Field Noise: Slight differences in areas that should be identical. For example, "blotchiness" in the background behind a title. Although often not objectionable to the human eye, "flat field" noise degrades compression and may be removed with the Adaptive Noise Reduction filter.

Flat Projection: Applies maps to surfaces in a flat manner.

Flat Shading: This allows computers to create colored solid objects instead of wireframe models. Flat shading colors every polygon in a 3D object the same color, which is varied based on its orientation to a light source. When the polygon or surfaces making up the 3D object are small enough, flat shading can provide some realism.

Flattening: The final pass applied to a QuickTime movie, which ensures that the movie data is laid out in a completely linear fashion, and all external references are removed. It also ensures that the sound is interleaved properly with the video.

Flattening (new): Resolving all references to data, whether internal or external, making a movie self-contained, deleting any un-referenced sample data, making multiple copies of any data referenced multiple times, and interleaving the data for smooth playback.

Flattening (old): In QuickTime 1.0, a movie's sample data was stored in the resource fork; it was necessary to flatten the movie by putting everything into the data fork to make the movie cross-platform. QuickTime now stores everything in the data fork by default, so this meaning of "flattening" has become obsolete.

FLC: See Ferroelectric Liquid Crystals.

FLI: An animation file. The structure is very similar to that of a FLC file; however they are different file formats. An "FLI" file has the extension ".fli"

Flipbook: A small booklet of sequential drawings that appear to move when thumbed

flipbook

---

through. Invented in 1868 the flipbook was originally called kineography.

FLIP: A method used by animators to check the effect of their work at the pencil stage. The drawings are held at the top with one hand and released sequentially with the thumb and forefinger of the other.

Floating Palettes: Groups of icons that perform functions; usually grouped together and can be freely positioned on the screen with a graphical user interface.

Flowcharts: In an interactive design, a map of the user's options and corresponding responses to input.

Flying Logo: A general class of broadcast 3D graphics. The name given often to a 3D corporate logo that is animated to appear as if it were flying through an environment.

FM Synthesis: Low-end sound cards create computerized tones using FM (frequency modulation). The result sounds very unmusical, computer-generated.

Focal Distance: The distance between the camera and the subject.

Focal Length: The relation between the near clipping plane and the far clipping plane.

Focal Length Equivalency: A digicam lens specs are frequently stated in this term. For example, a digicam lens that zooms from 9.2 mm to 28 mm would be described as 36 mm to 110 mm (equiv).

Fogging: Creates a fog-like effect by placing a haze over the scene; used to make objects appear slowly to avoid their sudden appearance.

Foley: Named after Inventor Jack Foley, the art of creating and recording sound effects in synch to the picture during post-production.

Font: A complete set of characters in a particular size and style of type, including the letter set, number set, and all of the special character and diacritical marks made by pressing the shift, option or command/control keys.

Footage: A method used to measure film length and screen time. As 90 feet of 35 mm film equals one minute of screen time, 35 mm footage is used in many studios as a measure of an animator's weekly output.

Footcandle: The standard measurement of a light's intensity as it illuminates an object's surface.

Force Feedback: Representations of the inertia or resistance objects have when moved or touched.

Forced Perspective: A technique that is employed by architectural miniature model makers or 3D artist to exaggerate the perspective of objects in an environment. For example buildings in the background are made disproportionately smaller to increase the distance with that of the foreground buildings. This is often done to create a more realistic image on film.

Forces: Gravity and winds, for example, both local (fan) and global. This force intensity, direction, etc. may be animated.

Foreground Color: Applied when a painting tool is used, type is created, or the stroke command is applied.

Form Factors: The name for the illumination coupling factors between polygons used in radiosity. Each form factor indicates the amount of light that one polygon will extend to another polygon.

Formation: The trademark of Will Vinton Studio, a stop-motion animation technique that uses a Styrofoam as the raw material for creating a 3D character.

Formats: Any method of arranging data for storage or display.

Forms: HTML tags that define and label text-entry boxes, check boxes, radio buttons, and/or drop-down menus to create on-screen forms used to collect information.

Forward Kinematics: The angles of the joints are manipulated to achieve a specific motion.

Four-Color Process Printing: The basic method of recreating a broad spectrum of colors on a printing press.

FOV: See Field of View.

FOVg: See Geometric Field of View.

FPS: See Frames Per Second.

Fractal: Very complex pictures generated by a computer from a single formula— often very colorful. Using iterations, meaning that one formula is repeated with slightly different values repeatedly, accounting for the results from the previous iteration, creates a fractal.

Fractal Compression: Compression technique that reduces images to a series of fractal-based formulas for very high-compression levels.

Fractal Graphics: Irregular, often organic shapes that occur in nature.

Fractal Image Format: See FIF.

Fractal Media: Works that use fractal algorithms.

Fractal Procedures: Procedures that divide the polygons in the object recursively and randomly into many irregular shapes resembling those found in nature.

Fragmented File: A file that has been written to a disk in discontinuous sectors.

Frame: The smallest unit of animation or an individual photograph on a strip of film. The term comes from movie and video production and frames of films.

Frame Buffer: A part of the memory used to store the actual calculated frame. It delivers smooth animation usually stores two frames: one being calculated by the 3D accelerator, while the second is being sent to the monitor. Also known as Double Buffering.

Frame Grabber: A card that captures a single frame from a video stream and stores it as a still image.

Frames Per Second (FPS): The number of still frames (pictures) that give the illusion of motion, which appear in a single second of time.

Frame Rate: The number of images per second displayed in a stream of video.

Frame-By-Frame: Filming in which each frame is exposed separately, as the object being photographed must be altered before each exposure in order to create the illusion of movement in the finished film.

Freeform Extrusion: An extrusion that takes place along several axes.

Freeform Lattice: A 3D grid of points and lines that controls the points of a 3D model.

Freeform Modeling: Modeling used when other modeling techniques are too rigid for building a specific scene, or when using a combination of other tools might do the job but might also require additional production time and a larger production budget.

Freeform Shape Animation: Animation created first by placing two versions of a 3D polygonal or spline-based model in each of two contiguous key frames, and then modifying the shape of one of the two models by pulling the points in the planar or curved mesh that define it.

Freelance: Work performed on a contractual, or assignment basis, rather than on-staff.

Freeware: Software developed and released to the public at no charge, and cannot be resold or relabeled without the consent of the originator. See also Shareware and Public Domain.

Freeze-Frame: A single-frame or image display held motionless—selected from video or film footage.

Fresnel: An enclosed lighting element designed for maximum light control.

Fringing: A video term for a line of incorrect color that appears between two colors.

Front Plane: The XZ axes define the top plane, and the YZ axes define the side plane.

Front Projection:

Frontal Light at the Subject's Level: A lighting technique that tends to flatten the subject.

Frontal Light From Below: A lighting technique that is effective for casting pronounced shadows both on the subject and the environment.

Front-End: The part of a display controller that receives drawing commands from the processor and writes the primitives into the bitmap.

Full Animation: Animation that depicts movement and character as completely and smoothly as possible, giving 3D illusions of weight and motion.

Full Frame: This term refers to the way in which video images are captured. A full frame occurs when one image equals two fields alternated inside the image file to produce one full frame.

Full-Motion Video: Digital video running at 30 fps (NTSC: US standard) that does not necessarily fill the screen.

Full-Screen Video: Digital video filling the entire screen (typically 640x480 pixels).

Function Curve: The timing (speed) of animation is controlled by function curves— the steeper the curve the faster the animation. Flat Fcurve results in no animation. Also known as Fcurve or Animation curve.

Futz: The process of altering the tone of a sound to make it seem as if it is coming from the radio or television set.

Fuzzy Logic: Computer-based circuitry that is able to use successive approximation to arrive at a result when no clear-cut answer is otherwise attainable.

G

Gag: Trade jargon for a funny situation in a story.

Gamma: A measure of contrast that affects the middle tones in an image. Also the numerical value of the exponent to which a video signal is raised by a power function to obtain linear-light. This may also be a term used when discussing the measure of light and dark in a CRT display.

Gamma Correction: A process that corrects the visual display based on the difference between the way light is recorded and displayed.

Gamut: The range of possible colors within a given color space. For example, the gamut of NTSC is dramatically more limited than the gamut of the RGB color space.

Gateway: A dedicated computer that connects two or more networks and routes information between them.

Gauge: A term that refers to the format of the film stock. For example, super-8, 16 mm, or 35 mm.

Gaussian Blur: A blurring filter that can be adjusted to provide very high levels of blurring.

Gaze Direction: The direction the virtual camera is pointed in the scene description. The center of the image will display whatever is along the gaze direction from the eye point.

General MIDI: An emerging standard for MIDI (Musical Instrument Digital Interface).

Generation Loss: The loss in image clarity when one analog videotape recording is copied to another. The decrease of clarity occurs as a result of decreasing signal-to-noise ratio.

Generations: The number of times a video piece has been re-recorded.

Genre: The category of the story being told. For example, a comedy, a western, a mystery, etc.

Geometric Field of View (FOVg): The angle, in degrees, of the computed visual scene. Most HMDs offer 60 to 90 degrees FOV, but the scene can be computed to fit from 0 to 360 degrees field of view for any particular projection point. If FOVg is larger than the FOV, then objects will appear pin-cushioned and distorted; if FOVg is smaller than the FOV, then objects will appear barreled and distorted.

Geometric Primitives: A collection of tools provided by computer programs for creating simple shapes.

Geometric Transformations: The functions used for modifying the shape of objects, their size and proportions, as well as their positions in space.

Geometry File: Files that contain the data describing the object.

Gesture: A hand motion that can be interpreted as a sign or signal.

Giclee: A work of art created to benefit fine-art printing—a fine-art Giclee is created from the artist's original artwork. An extremely high-resolution digital image of the artwork is made then loaded into specially enhanced printers that output the digital image onto fine-art paper or canvas. Since the digital image includes every subtlety and nuance of the original, the fine-art Giclee is often indistinguishable from the original work of art.

GIF (Graphics Interchange Format): Along with the jpg format, a widely-used method of compressing photo and illustration data for Internet use.

GIF Animation: A simple, affordable way to create "instant animation," allowing a limited form of sprite-based animation.

Gigabyte: A unit of computer storage representing one billion bytes.

Glass Shot: A traditional film technique whereby an image is painted on a glass sheet and is filmed simultaneously with the set. This technique is traditionally used for painting large background scenes such as landscapes on a movie studio set.

Global Illumination: Rendering techniques that account for natural lighting.

Global Key: A keyboard character that performs a specific global function.

Global transformations: Transformations that are applied to objects using the environment's axes or origin.

Glow: The opposite of a shadow—it creates a surrounding highlight of an image. A high radiance creates a soft, subtle glow, while a low radiance creates a hard, bright glow, such as neon.

Goggles: Often used in reference to Head Mounted Displays or other displays.

Gold Master: A copy of the entire source material of a new media project from which duplicates can be mass-produced.

Go-Motion: A technique create by Industrial Light and Magic that permits them to shot single frames of miniatures

---

in motion. This results in motion blurred still shots. The motion blur create a more realistic smooth motion that is not found in traditional stop-motion techniques.

Good Take: A scene that has been approved by the director.

GOP (Group of Pictures): A self-contained sequence of MPEG frames starting with an I-frame, followed by B- and P-frames, and ending with a P-frame.

Gopher: A menu-driven system allowing one to search for and retrieve files from the Net.

Gouraud Shading: Shading polygons smoothly with bilinear interpolation. A method of shading 3D objects invented by Henri Gouraud in 1971, it creates the appearance of a curved surface by interpolating the color across the polygons, providing a dramatic increase in rendering quality.

Gradient: A gradual transition of colors. For example, metallic images are gradients. Web images that use gradient fills as a special effect should be saved in a JPEG rather than a GIF format.

Gradient Fill: An enhancement to the fill tool that fills an area with a gradual transition from one color to another.

Graftals (Database Amplification): A technique that allows the creation of complex images from small databases.

Graphic Backgrounds: The bottom-most layer on a Web page, usually with a design or color that highlights the above copy. A small graphic can be tiled to create a background texture for a Web page.

Graphic Primitive: An object that the graphics system is capable of drawing into the bitmap. For example, lines, points, and some polygons.

Graphical User Interface (GUI): A computer interface based on pictures rather than text. Windows, Macintosh, Netscape and Mosaic are examples of GUI products.

Graphics: The visual content prepared for a production.

Graphics Accelerator: A graphics card used in animation production/creation to speed the display/preview of 3D animation.

Graphics Bitmap: Images that are laid out in pixels, much like dots of paint on a canvas. Bitmap objects are not independent entities, which can be singled out for manipulation, but a patterned series of dots. To enlarge (or reduce) bitmap images, the number of pixels is increased (decreased), often giving the resulting image a jagged appearance. Scanners produce bitmap images (.TIF), as does Windows' Paint Brush (.BMP, .PCX); bitmaps are one of the most commonly compatible types of image formats.

Graphics Interchange Format: See GIF.

Graphics Vector: Graphics consisting of objects, each of which can be separately manipulated. For example, sized, moved, (un) grouped and positioned to the back/front. The graphic components are calculated for size without distortion. File formats include: AutoCAD DXF, CBM, EPS, HGL, PIC, DRW, WMF, and WPG.

Graphing: To outline a cartoon or script, scene-by-scene, listing the essence of each scene, who is in the scene, where and when the scene takes place, and what time the scene falls in the episode (by minutes) or script (by page).

Grayscale: An application of black ink (for print) or the color black (for the screen) that simulates a range of tones. Grayscale images have no hue (color).

Grayscale Image: An image consisting of up to 256 levels of gray with eight bits of color data per pixel.

Green Screen: The same as blue screen. Green screen is often used because the grain of the color green is finer than the color blue, resulting in a better composite.

Grip: In a film or video production, the person who mounts or positions the camera according to the director's instructions.

Group of Pictures: See GOP.

GUI: See Graphical User Interface.

Gum Arabic Based Cel Paints: The most common type of paint once used at various studios was a rewet table, opaque watercolor with a gum Arabic binder. Some studios bought ready-made paint, but MGM and Disney custom manufactured their own paints in-house. Although most studios abandoned this type of paint in the early 1960s when synthetic binders were introduced, the Disney Studios continued to manufacture and use it in production until *The Great Mouse Detective* was released in 1986.

H

Hacker: A person who has developed sophisticated computer-programming skills to break codes and access restricted data without access privileges.

Half Horizontal Resolution: See HHR.

Halftone: The screening of a continuous-tone image into small dots of varying sizes.

Haloing: A term used to describe the separation of the plastic laminate around the perimeter of a character—common in cels of this type.

Hand Inking: Prior to the late 1950s, all animation drawings were hand-traced onto cels using a quill pen or brush. A variety of inks were used, but in general, the colored ink lines were simply cel paint thinned down to the proper consistency. Hand inking is still widely used in animated commercials, special effects shots, and in publicity artwork.

Hand-Inked Cel: A Cel that has had the animation drawing traced onto it by hand in different color inks.

Hand-Inked-Line Cel: Cels recreated by Disney using the traditional animation techniques, including tracing an animation drawing onto acetate by hand with different color inks, and hand-painting it with gum-based or acrylic-based colors.

Handles: In many applications when a graphical object is selected, an outline of the object appears with small boxes, each of which is a handle. Dragging the handles will change the shape and size of the object.

Hand-Painted Background: A type of presentation background generally painted recently for the purpose of displaying a cel—not a production background.

Hand-Prepared Background: A non-production background prepared by a studio artist to enhance or complete a cel setup.

Hanging Minitures: Miniatures that are suspended between the lens and a full-size set in such a way that miniature and full-size components are filmed simultaneously, with the result that they seem to be continuous parts of a single entity.

Hang Time: A term that refers to when a cartoon character races off a cliff and "hangs" in mid-air.

Haptic Interfaces: Interfaces that use all the physical sensors that provide a sense of touch at the skin level and force feedback information from muscles and joints.

Hard Copy: Documents and images in printed, concrete form, such as slides, printed, transparencies, and plots.

Hardware: The electromechanical segment of a data processing system.

HDTV: See High Definition Television.

Head: A mathematical transformation of sound spectrum that modifies the amplitude and phase of acoustic signals to take into account the shape effects of the listener's head.

Head-Coupled: Display or robotic actions that are activated by head motion through a head-tracking device.

Head Tracking: The process of monitoring the position of the head with various devices.

Header: In telecommunications and computing, the information recorded at the beginning of a transmitted data packet, which may identify what will follow.

Head Mounted Display (HMD): A headset used with virtual reality systems. Can be a pair of goggles or a full helmet— in front of each eye is a tiny monitor displaying real-time 3D images. Most HMDs include a head tracker so that the system can respond to head movements.

Heads Up Display (HUD): A display device allowing users to see graphics superimposed on their view of the world. (Created for aviators to see symbols and dials while looking out the window.)

Hexadecimal: Used to color Web pages, a numbering system that uses a base of 16. The first ten digits are 0-9, and the next six are A-F.

HHR (Half Horizontal Resolution): MPEG-2 files may be stored at half-normal horizontal resolution to create lower data rate files. When displayed, the video is "stretched" by the MPEG player to full resolution.

Hi8: A video format invented by Sony to offer a higher consumer grade resolution than regular camcorder 8mm videotape.

Hidden File: A file whose attributes are set so that it is not normally shown in a directory listing.

Hidden Surface: The parts of a graphics object occluded by intervening objects.

Hidden-Line Removal: Displays portions of a wireframe model that faces the camera.

Hidden-Surface Removal: Determines which surfaces are visible and which are not.

Hidden-Surface/Hidden-Line Algorithm: An algorithm used to determine which surfaces are "behind" a 3D object from the viewer's perspective, and thus should be "hidden" when the computer renders a 3D image.

Hierarchical Structures: Groups of 3D objects linked in the form of parent and child relationships. For example in the hierarchical structure of a humanlike arm model the arm is the parent, the forearm and hand are children of the arm. If the parent is moved the children will move along with the arm as one.

hierarchical structure

High Color: A video/PC term used to describe 16-bit color depth.

High Sierra: The original file system standard developed for CD-ROM, later modified and adopted as ISO 9660. A format in which files and directories are placed on CD-ROM.

High/Low Resolution: The number of pixels-per-inch (or centimeter) or the depth of color measurement. The higher the resolution of an image, the closer to photo quality and the larger the file.

High-Angle Shot: A camera's view looking down at the point of interest.

High-Concept: A story idea that can be conveyed in one or two sentences with a hook, making the story easily recognized as able to become a profitable cartoon series.

High-Contrast Masks: Sharp edges and solid areas.

Highlights: The lightest area of an image drawing or model. The area of a subject that receives the most illumination.

Highpass Filter: A circuit that passes frequencies above a specific frequency (the cutoff frequency); frequencies below the cutoff frequency are reduced in amplitude to be eliminated.

Histogram: A 2D graphic representation of the pixel value distribution of an image; the horizontal coordinate is the pixel value, whereas the vertical coordinate represents the numbers of pixels at a given value.

HLS (Hue, Lightness, Saturation): A color model based on the hue, saturation, and lightness of a color.

HMD: See Head-Mounted Display.

Hold: To freeze or stop the action; the same cel or position of an object is photographed for several frames.

Holodeck: A virtual reality simulation system and location used primarily for entertainment by the crew of the "Enterprise in Star Trek: The Next Generation" television series.

Hologram: An image with a layered, 3D appearance produced by a laser-based system rather than a lens.

HOM: See Hall of Mirrors.

Homage: Usually a respectful tribute to someone. In the movies, this can often occur when within one movie reference is made to another.

HOOD: A swinging wrap-around display used in place of Head Mounted Display.

Hook: A twist that makes the story idea fresh and original.

Host: A computer that acts as a file server; users at remote computers (i.e., client computers) may access information stored on the server or host computer.

Hot Spot: An area of a cel that is reflecting lights back into the camera, causing that spot to be overexposed.

HSB (Hue, Saturation, and Brightness): A color model based on the hue, saturation, and brightness of a color.

HSV (Hue, Saturation, and Value): Color space that defines colors in terms of their hue (the color of an object, such as green), saturation (how much gray is in the color), and value (the lightness or darkness of the color). Variations on this color space include HSB (Hue, Saturation, Brightness) and HSL (Hue, Saturation, Lightness).

HTML (HyperText Markup Language): A set of commands used to mark documents capable of being read by a Web browser.. Tags placed in a text document that provides directions for a Web browser to read it.

HTTP (HyperText Transfer Protocol): The most common transfer protocol used on the Web.

HUD: See Heads Up Display.

Hue: The actual color of an object. Hue is measured as a location on a color wheel, expressed in degrees. It is also understood as the names of specific colors, like blue, red, yellow, etc.

Huffman Compression: A method of compressing graphics data files.

HWB: Hue, Whiteness, and Blackness.

Hybrid Disc: A CD-ROM in the logical disc format, containing ISO 9660.

Hyperlink: An electronic connection from a Web page to either (1) other Web pages on the same site, or (2) Web pages located on another site. It's also a connection between one hypertext document page to another. Also known as Link.

Hypermedia: New media or digital media that refers to a dimensional environment with text, graphics, audio, animation, and video elements. Also known as Multimedia.

Hypertext: "Text" that allows users to "hyper-jump"; similar to regular text, with one exception: hypertext contains connections within the text to other Web documents. The connections are usually denoted as underlined, colored text. The "documents" to which the hypertext connects may be local or remote.

HyperText Markup Language: See HTML.

HyperText Transfer Protocol: See HTTP.

Hysterical Sublime: An encounter with information stimuli that is beyond comprehension.

I

I/O (Input/Output): An alternate term for scanning and recording.

IBM MicroDrive: A high-capacity (up to one gigabyte) spinning storage device that can be used with digicams accepting Compact Flash II memory cards.

IC: See Integrated Circuit.

ICC: International Color Consortium.

Icons: Small graphics symbols used to represent programs, data, or other functions within a graphical user interface.

Icosahedron: A twenty-sided rectangular polyhedral.

ICR (Intelligent Character Recognition): A scanning device/process for hand-print recognition.

iDCT (Inverse Discrete Cosine Transform): The mathematical algorithm used to decode MPEG video; often built into hardware.

IDE (Integrated Device Electronics): An inexpensive, popular interface for PC hardware and devices; IDE has largely supplanted EIDE and SCSI.

I-Frame: Complete MPEG frame containing entire image. Similar to "key frame" in QuickTime/AVI. See also Intraframe.

IHS (Intensity, Hue, and Saturation): An area wherein colors are defined by their intensity, hue, and saturation attributes; sometimes referred to as HSV, which stands for Hue, Saturation, and Value.

Illegal Colors: Colors reaching beyond the bounds of a system's color range.

IMA: A ratio of 4:1 compression audio codec that works with 16-bit audio. IMA is also a standard created by the Interactive Multimedia Association.

Image: A 2D array of pixels forming a picture.

Image Map: A single graphic image containing multiple links.

Image Processing: The capture and manipulation of images in order to enhance or extract information.

Image Resolution: The amount of data stored in an image file, measured in pixels-per-inch (ppi).

Image Size: The size, in inches, of the character(s).

Image Space: A method of hidden surface removal; retains the depth information of the objects in the scene, but sorts from a lateral position, and only to the resolution of the display device.

Imagesetter: A high-resolution printer (usually 1,270-4,000 dpi) that generates paper or film output from a computer file.

Immersion: The cognitive conviction or feeling of presence surrounded by space, and capable of interacting with all available objects within a VR setting.

Import Filters: Tables that instruct the conversion utility program to translate each of the elements encountered in the original or foreign file.

Impressionists: A 19th-century group of artists whose paintings captured color and mood, rather than exact perspective outlines.

In-betweener: A person whose function it is to draw in-between drawings—usually a novice.

In-Betweens: Drawings between the extreme points of movement.

Incidentals Light: Light shining directly on a surface.

Inclusive Link: A link that allows local light source to always illuminate the objects linked to it, as well as other objects in the scene that may be directly exposed to it.

Indeo: Several codecs developed by Intel that allow temporal and spatial compression, as well as data-rate limiting.

Indexed Color: In Photoshop, an image mode in which there is only one channel and a color table containing up to 256 colors. All colors in an Indexed Color image are displayed on its table—unlike an image in any other mode.

Info-Lithium: A battery that indicates its remaining shooting time in minutes on the digicam's LCD Monitor screen.

Information Page: A static Web page designed, coded, and written for optimal search engine and directory positioning.

Infotainment: Interactive CD-ROM programs that blend entertainment with informational, educational activities.

Infrared: A spectrum of electromagnetic radiation with wavelengths longer than visible light waves, but shorter than microwaves.

Inker's Test/Clean-Up Tests: Beginning inkers and assistant animators were often given scenes of animation from previous productions to practice on. Also, this category of art encompasses test pieces given to prospective employees to judge their level of skill.

Inkjet: A type of printing in which dots of ink are sprayed onto paper to create the image. Some inkjet printers can lay down 1,440 dots of ink per inch, resulting in photo-quality prints (provided that the image has adequate resolution in pixels to begin with).

Inline: To view within the browser page, rather needing an external application to view.

Input/Output: See I/O.

Inside of the Mat Opening: See IOM.

Inspirational Drawing: See Concept Drawing.

Instancing: Creates multiples of the original object by using its numerical description and cloning it elsewhere in the scene. Also known as Cloning.

Instructional Design: Computer-aided methods of presenting material that result in learning.

Instructional Designer: An educational training developer.

INT (Interior): A term that describes the location and inner area.

Integrated Circuit (IC): A very small electronic component consisting of scores of transistors, resistors, capacitors and diodes all in one sealed housing.

Integrated Device Electronics: See IDE.

Integrated Services Digital Network: See ISDN.

Intellectual Property: Content or knowledge that may be protected by copyright.

Intelligent Character Recognition: See ICR.

Intensity: The brightness of a light source as measured in foot-candles or lux.

Interactive: The ability to be modified or affected by a user.

Interactive Art: Art that requires input (from audience or environment) in order to function.

Interactive Camera Placement: The process of finding a camera position.

Interactive Fiction: Dramatic creations that encourage user and viewer participation through computer technology. For example, hypertext, group feedback, or VR.

Interactive Media: Types of media allowing users to control the flow of program material.

Interactive Services: Services that allow subscribers to send messages to a programming source, or content provider, to control the flow of information and engage in two-way communications.

Interactive Television: A system with the capacity to send information to a broadcast television provider via another communications device, such as a telephone, keypad, or touch screen, allowing viewers to send messages back to the televised source.

Interactivity: The base of the dialog established between the system and the individuals using it.

Interaural Amplitude: The differences between two ears in the intensity of sound.

Interaural Time: The differences between two ears in phase of sound.

Interface: The representation of images, text, and objects that enable interaction with software. This term also describes the connection between two hardware devices allowing the exchange of data.

Interface Design: A term that refers to the graphical conventions such as the shape of icons, typography and color, as well as with the sequencing of events, selection techniques, and interplay of sound, text, and images.

Interframe: In QuickTime, temporally compressed frame. For example, MPEG has two types of interframes: "B-frames" and "P-frames." Also known as Difference or Delta Frame.

Interframe Compression: Compression between video frames accomplished by storing a whole frame, then just small pieces (areas of change) for the next several frames, rather than storing complete image after complete image. Storing each frame as a whole image may include redundant video information, resulting in larger file size.

Interlace: Storing partial data from a single graphic image in multiple sequences. The purpose is to create a partial image appearing on-screen, rather than having to wait for the entire image to appear. Interlace also describes equally spaced sets of lines from the original image are stored together, which appear atop one another in sequence.

Interleaving: Intermixing video and audio data in the final file. Interleaving is required for proper playback of movies because it allows the drive to read the file in a linear fashion and receive the separate audio and video data as needed.

Interlock: A system that electronically links a projector with a sound recorder. It's used during post-production to view the edited film and soundtrack, to check timing, pacing, and synchronization, etc.

Intermedia: Art that transcends the object, including installations, slide projections, 16 mm films, and performances.

Inter-Negative: A negative made directly from the original film.

Internet: A global system of computer networks allowing users to access information on, and transmit information to, any other computer on the network. The Internet originally developed from the ARPAnet model, which specifies that communication occurs between the source and destination computer in small parcels of data known as Internet Protocol (IP) packets. Also known as "The Network of Networks," "The Information Highway," and "The World Wide Web (www)."

Internet Protocol (IP): The protocol that provides addresses needed to move packets of information across networks. IP addresses contain two parts: A network identifier and a host identifier.

Internet Relay Chat (IRC): A mechanism that allows for a number of Internet users to connect to the same network node and chat in real time. An IRC server is necessary to access this feature.

Internet Service Provider (ISP): A company that provides access to the Internet, sometimes with e-mail or other services, and usually for a fee.

Internet Studio: A Web programming language developed by Microsoft that uses drag-and-drop and OLE, not HTML, to publish Web pages.

Interpolated Shading: In this process, illumination values are calculated at the polygon vertices and are used to interpolate the pixel values in between.

Interpolation: The process of adding or subtracting pixels to an image (usually in an imaging program) to increase or reduce its size at a desired resolution. Also known as Resampling or Upsampling, and Downsampling.

Interrupt: A computer instruction that momentarily stops the regular operation of a routine.

Interstitial: A Web advertisement that appears in a separate browser window than the target Web page.

Intraframe: A spatially compressed frame from which interframes are based. Also known as Key Frame in QuickTime and I-frame in MPEG.

Intraframe Coding: Related to video compression, a technique that allocates more data to the coding of highly detailed parts of a single frame at the expense of less-detailed areas.

Intranet: A private network within a company or organization for internal use only. An intranet is a communications and productivity tool utilizing standard Internet protocols and technologies (TCP/IP, HTTP, and HTML, search engines, etc.) within an organization or company, allowing employees to connect and enable them to easily access company resources using standard Internet browsers, cutting costs, and enhancing productivity.

Inverse Discrete Cosine Transform: See iDCT.

Inverse Dynamics: A method used to specify motion in an animation. Linkages and other constraints are defined for the objects. A final state is then specified for some of the objects, and the computer calculates the motion of all the objects so that the final state is reached. Unlike in inverse kinematics, dynamic properties are taken into account, such as momentum, friction, energy loss in collisions, etc.

Inverse Kinematics: This term determines the motion of entire skeletons based on the final angles of the key joints that define the motion.

Invert Filter: A filter that inverts the pixel values of an image, creating a negative.

IOM (Inside of the Mat Opening): IOM measurement is used when a frame or mat makes measurement of the full object impossible.

IP: See Internet Protocol.

IPIX: A technology developed by Interactive Pictures Corporation (formerly known as OmniView) that allows users to create and view 360-degree panoramic photographs. Originally called PhotoBubble, IPIX images are created by stitching together two hemispherical shots taken through a fish-eye lens. The result is a spherical panoramic image.

IRC: See Internet Relay Chat.

Iris: Like the iris of the eye, a valve within a lens to control the amount of light that passes through. Opening the iris permits more light to pass through the lens and closing the iris less. The degree to which the iris is open or closed is measured in F-stops, and on some lenses supplemented by T-Stops.

Iris-In: A shot that opens from darkness in an expanding circle of light.

Iris-Out: The opposite of an iris-in.

Iris Wipe: A wipe effect in the form of an expanding or diminishing circle.

ISDN (Integrated Services Digital Network): A network/telephone connection that transfers data at rates more than four times faster than a 28.8 kbps modem. Ordinary modems (non-ISDN) convert computer data to audio tones/analog to transfer via the phone lines. ISDN "modems" connect digitally.

ISO 9660: The international standard for the file system used by CD-ROM. Allows file names of only 8 characters plus a 3-character extension.

ISO Equivalency: A measure of the digicam's sensitivity to light using conventional film speeds as a yardstick. Most digicams have fixed ISO equivalents, while others can be set to sensitivities, ranging from 80—640, to achieve adequate exposure under different lighting conditions.

ISO: International Standards Organization.

Isochronous: A term that describes types of data transmission in which characters are separated by a whole number of bit-length intervals.

ISP: See Internet Service Provider.

Iteration: The process of repeating the design and development process until satisfied**.**

ITS: International Teleproduction Society.

J

Jack: To connect to the matrix of virtual space.

Jaggies: The undesirable artifacts that appear in a graphic display or printout resulting from lack of adequate resolution.

JAVA: A simple programming language developed by Sun Microsystems designed for writing programs that can be easily downloaded and immediately run by a Web browser.

JAVA Applets: Small programs written in JAVA producing various special effects, which are embedded directly into the Web pages; applets automatically download with the page. Browsers such as HotJava or Netscape 2.0 (available at UNCG) are needed to view applet pages.

JAVA Beans: A component API's allowing Java applications built to run in other frameworks; i.e., Microsoft Word.

JAVA Script: A scripting language developed by Netscape that make Web pages more animated and dynamic in terms of graphics and navigation. One of the most common graphic Javascript effects is called a mouseover, and Javascript navigation is commonly created using drop-down menus.

Jewel Cases: Plastic carrying cases for CDs.

Jitter: A shift in phase of digital pulses in transmission, causing lack of synchronization.

Jitterbuster: A device, such as Monarchy Audio's Digital Interface Processor, that seeks to suppress jitters, or flickering signals, in audio transmissions.

Jog: To change positions within a video clip, or shuttle it by a single frame or small number of frames.

Joint: The point where two or more bones are joined.

Joint Photographic Experts Group: See JPEG.

Joystick: An input device that rotates an axis and controls the position of a cursor.

joystick

JPEG (Joint Photographic Experts Group): A file format used to create full-color and black-and-white graphic images. JPEG images allow for more colors than GIF images, and are usually smaller in size.

Juxtapose: To place side-by-side in comparison.

K

Key Drawing: A drawing showing the most indicative pose in a scene.

Key Frame Animation: An animation control method that works by specifying the scene state at selected, or key, frames. The scene state for the remaining frames is interpolated from the state at the key frames.

Key Frame: A complete video frame, containing all the image detail.

Key Framing: A term used to define an animated sequence based on its key moments.

Key Lights: Light sources used to illuminate the main action area.

Key Master Background: Another name for Matching Background.

Key Master Setup: Cel(s) with their original matching background that can be cued up in the film layout; detailed drawings depicting master scenes for a sequence often showing master background, camera movements, and placement of characters.

Key: The process of superimposing video from one source atop another.

Key Pose: The characteristic or main pose in a movement.

Keyboard: A device that contains alphanumeric, symbolic, and function keys used to input text or instructions to a computer.

Keypad: A small keyboard typically consisting of numeric and function keys only.

Keywords: Words written in a high-level computing language that call subroutines.

kHz (kilohertz): An audio sample frequency unit of measure.

Kid-Relatable: A script written so as to be relatable to children.

Kilobit (Kb): A unit of measure for computer data. A Kilobit (with "K" and "b") is 1,024 bits, and rarely used.

Kilobyte: A unit of storage that represents 1,000 bytes.

Kilohertz: See kHz.

Kinaesthetic Dissonance: Mismatch between feedback or its absence from touch or motion during VR experiences.

Kinematics: The hierarchical relationship of various parts of objects that move. For example, shaking someone's hand will usually also move their wrist, forearm, elbow, and upper arm.

Kineography: See Flip Book.

Kinetic Art: Art consisting of moving parts.

Kiosk: A booth providing a computer-related service, often with a touch-screen. For example, an ATM, a tourist information stand, or a non-keyboard Web interface.

Knee Shot: A shot that presents character from the knees up.

Knots: Determines the distribution and local density of points on a curve.

Kodak Photo CD: Photographs/images are "printed"/digitized on CDs. The Photo CD comes with a contact sheet, and additional pictures can be added; to view the CD images, a viewer is needed. Also known as PCD.

Kps (Kilobits Per Second): A term for data rate meaning either Kilobytes or kilobits per second.

L

LAB: A 3D color model combining RGB and CMYK color spaces.

Laboratory: A facility that specializes in processing and printing film, sometimes offering additional services such as editing and film storage.

Lag: The delay between an action and its visual, acoustic, or other sensory feedback, often because of inherent delays in the tracking devices, or in the computation of the scene.

Laminated: A cel that has been encapsulated in thermoset plastic. Courvoisier laminated many cels, as did the Disney Original Art program. The purpose of lamination is to protect the cel, keeping the paint from chipping or cracking.

Lamination: The process of "sandwiching" a cel between sheets of clear plastic in an effort to preserve it. See also Laminated.

LAN (Local Area Network): A privately operated communications system interconnecting computers and communications equipment over a limited geographic area, usually five miles or less. LAN's enable local resource sharing (printers, files, etc.).

Landscape: A camera shot with a rectangular aspect ratio usually in the horizontal orientation.

Laserdisc Player: Similar to a VCR, this device plays back analog video stored on laserdiscs.

Lasso: A selection tool in a paint or graphics program that allow the user to select irregular shapes.

Lateral Light at The Subject's Level: Lighting technique that is useful to increase the contrast between light and dark.

Lateral Light From Above and Behind: An effective way to outline the subject against the background.

Lateral Light From Above: A lighting technique with one light on the left and one on the right; creates an effect similar to the 45-degree spotlight pair.

Lathe: A popular sweeping variation. Also known as Revolve.

Lattices: Allows control of freeform deformations.

Layers: An image with information from one area of depth. Composites are made up of at least two layers. Often, a live-action layer is composited with layers consisting of computer-generated elements. A background layer may also be referred to as the plate.

Layouts: The drawings of backgrounds for each scene to later be rendered by the background artist.

Layouts Drawing: A detailed pencil drawing indicating the fielding, the character's action, or the design of the background that acts as the scenery behind the character; there are two types of layouts: Character Layout, which outlines the character's path of movement, expressions and action within the scene, and the Background Layout, which generally consists of a line drawing of the environment in which the character exists; used as reference by the animator and the background painter, respectively.

LBE: See Location-Based Entertainment.

LCD (Liquid Crystal Display): Panels connected to computers that allow the display to be projected on a screen.

LCD Monitor: The Liquid Crystal Display color screen on most digicams, usually 1.8 to 2.5 inches measured diagonally and used to check images after they are shot. The LCD monitor can also be used to frame pictures before they are taken and is usually more accurate than the optical viewfinder, though not as convenient to use.

Leader: Blank time (silence) inserted between songs.

Leading: The vertical spacing between lines of text.

Learnware: A term used to describe new-media products designed for education and training purposes.

Left-Handed Coordinate System: The Z-axis (depth) decreases as it nears.

Leica Reel: In early production stages, in order to get an impression of how a film would appear in its finished state, story paintings, depicting as closely as possible finished staging and color, were photographed and projected with the soundtrack—referred to as the Leica Reel.

Lens Aperture: Measured in f/stop units.

Lens Distortion: An abnormal rendering of lines in an image. This most commonly appears to bend inward (pincushion distortion) or outward (barrel distortion). Correctable by using a plug-in within an imaging program.

Lens Flare: An effect related to light glow. It simulates the refraction of light inside of a camera lens.

Letterbox: To add black bars to the tops and bottoms of images that have a different aspect ratio than the display monitor.

Level of Detail (LOD): A model of a particular resolution among a series of models of the same object. Multiple LODs are used to increase graphics performance by drawing simpler geometry when the object occupies fewer pixels on the screen. LOD selection can also be driven by graphics load, area-of-interest, or gaze direction.

Level of Illumination: See Shade.

Level of Recursion: The amount of subdivision is usually expressed in the form of a factor.

Level: Because individual elements or characters in a scene may move at different rates or be drawn by different animators, they may be put on separate cels for ease or economy of animation. The layers of cels are referred to as levels. Usually, the elements that move most frequently will be placed on the upper levels, making it easier for the camera operator to change them.

Library: In programming, a list of procedures and/or functions that can be accessed and implemented.

Licensing: Contracting for the right to perform, record, distribute and/or digitally transmit a copyrighted song or other work.

Lifting: The separation of the paint or ink from the cel, often caused by dehydration. Separated section appears to be discolored. Also known as Separation.

Light Attenuation: The property of light dimming with distance from the light.

Light Meter: A device for photographers giving a precise, numerical value that represents different characteristics of the incident light at any point in the 3D environment.

Light On Dark: An inking technique sometimes used to delineate very dark areas on a character, in which the ink lines are of slightly lighter color, adding definition and depth.

Light Pen: A stylus that controls the position of a cursor on a monitor.

Light Ray: A ray that is launched from a point on an object towards a light source. The ray is used to determine whether the light source is illuminating the point. If the ray reaches the light source without hitting anything, then the light source is illuminating the point.

Light Vector: A vector from a point on an object towards a light source. Light vectors are usually unitized before use; needed for each light source in computing the apparent color when the object's surface properties include diffuse or specular reflection.

Lightness: Apparent achromatic value of a reflecting surface.

Lightning: A luminous, high-current, electric discharge with a long path that flows between a cloud and the ground, between two clouds, or between two parts of the same cloud.

LI-ion: See Lithium-ion.

Limited Animation: A term used to describe animation in which full movement is not depicted, but which relies on key poses and the movement of only those portions of the character that are essential to the motion.

Limited Edition Cel: A non-production hand-painted cel produced in limited quantities and created as fine art specifically for collectors. Each cel is individually hand numbered, stamped with a seal of authenticity, placed on lithographic or photograph background, and in many cases signed by the original artist. Limited editions are easily identified by a designating fraction (47/250) located in the lower righthand corner.

Limited Edition Hand-Painted Cel: A cel created in very limited numbers using the same hand-painting technique as production cels; often signed by the artist or director.

Line: Defined by the XYZ location of its two endpoints.

Line Buffer: A line buffer is a memory buffer used to hold one line of video. For example, if the horizontal resolution of the screen is 640 pixels, and RGB is used as the color space, the line buffer would have to be 640 locations long by 3 bytes wide.

Line of Sight: A perpendicular line that travels away from the camera from the point of view to the point of interest.

Line Wear: Missing, broken, or smeared lines on either hand inked or Xeroxed cels.

Lineage: The transfer of attributes from one level of the plant to another at the time of branching.

Linear: A term that describes a medium in which content is arranged sequentially, and the user must move through the material in either forward or reverse motions without entry points or branching.

Linear Interpolation: Linear means that the values fall along a line from one known point to the next, which means the value changes a fixed amount for a fixed-sized step; sometimes the term "linear interpolation" is used to refer to "bi-linear interpolation." See also Interpolation.

Linear Lights: Lights that have length but no width, and can be scaled to any size.

Linear Spline: A series of straight lines connecting the control points.

Line-Out Jack: A jack used to bypass any amplifier built into the sound card allowing one to connect the sound card to an external amplified source.

Lines Per Inch: See LPI.

Lingo: A mid-level scripting language used to create interactive multimedia projects.

Link: A connection between two pieces of data, such as an icon and the information it represents.

Lip Sync: Lip Synchronization—the matching of the character's mouth movements to the recorded dialog on the sound track.

List: Categorized text that may be it bulleted, numbered or unnumbered. The default list bullets and numbers are black with no special effects. To make a bulleted list using graphic images as bullets, Web graphic designers use a table format.

Listserv/Mailing Lists: An electronic mail conferencing system—subscribers receive e-mail messages from all contributing members of that list, and can mail to the list e-mail address to have the message distributed to all subscribed members.

Lithium-ion (LI-ion): A long-lasting rechargeable battery used in some digicams.

Litho Background: A printed background used to accompany cels sold at Disneyland in the 50s, 60s and early 70s. Backgrounds from several films of the period were used, and did not necessarily match the cels with which they were sold.

Lithograph: Fine-art lithography utilizes a traditional printing process whereby the artist's original image is transferred onto stone or metal lithography plates, usually by hand or chemically. Each color must be separated from the original image then transferred to the stone or plate. Under very heavy pressure, each color is printed onto fine-art paper one color at a time. When all of the image's individual colors have been printed together onto the paper, the combined colors create the final product.

Live Action: Video that is filmed on location or in a studio containing real-world subjects. The term "live action video" is usually used to differentiate between real-world video and computer-generated video.

Live Control: Multiple layers of motion.

Local Area Network: See LAN.

Local Bus: In microcomputer architecture, a data bus with a short signal path between the main processor and I/O processors, frequently used for fast video functions.

Local Illumination: A way in which light is emitted, reflected and transmitted by a specific surface or light source.

Local Transformations: Transformations that are applied to a single object, or limited selection of objects, using its axes and origin.

Location-Based Entertainment (LBE): A VR game that involves a scenario based on another time and place; filling a studio or space with VR games.

Locking: The process of keeping an object's element from moving.

Lock-Off Camera: A term that refers to a camera placed in a fixed position to shoot a sequence, in order to more easily composite it with other elements, including computer-generated imagery.

LOD: See Level of Detail.

Logical Operators: Operators used to create models by adding and subtracting shapes in a variety of ways.

Long Shot (LS): A shot focused on scenery and hardly permits recognition of individual characters in an environment.

Looping: A process of replacing a portion of the recorded soundtrack that may be unclear or require changing.

Lossless Compression: In graphic design, a term that refers to a data compression technique in which the file quality is preserved and no data is lost; commonly used with GIF images, but can only reduce file size to about half of its original size.

Lossy Compression: A method of compressing images by throwing away unneeded data. It's a one-way process: converting the compressed file back to the original format will result in a file with missing information that may or may not significantly affect the quality of the reconverted file. For example, MP3—WAV files created from MP3 files will not sound quite as full or rich as the original WAV files used to create the MP3 files.

Low-Angle Shot: A camera placed below the point of interest.

Lowpass Filter: A circuit that passes frequencies below a specific frequency (the cutoff frequency). Frequencies above the cutoff frequency are reduced in amplitude to be eliminated.

LPCM: See Linear PCM.

LPI (Line Per Inch): A measure of resolution often used to describe screens.

LPTV: Low-power TV.

LS: See Long Shot.

L-Systems: A term created by Lindenmayer Systems defined as structure-oriented models describing the growth process of a plant at the level of cellular interaction.

Luminance: A color's brightness.

Luminance Signal: The monochrome (b/w) portion of the video signal, describing brightness and contrast.

Lux: The measurement of a light's intensity.

LZW Compression (Lempel-Ziv and Welch): A digital data compression scheme that works by identifying and compressing recurring patterns in the data.

M

Mach Bands: An optical illusion caused by a sudden change in the rate of brightness change (discontinuities in the brightness' second derivative), giving the appearance of a light or dark line at the sudden change.

Macro: The ability of a lens to focus inches away from an object/subject to produce close-ups, sometimes even larger-than-life-size.

Macroblock: In MPEG compression (and other inter-frame compression methods) each frame is broken into a grid— each piece of the grid is called a macroblock. When motion occurs in very low bit rate MPEG videos, the macroblocks are visible (when the picture gets very blocky) because there are not enough bits to make each block accurately represent its piece of the picture.

Magic Wand: A painting tool that selects any range of similar, adjoining colors.

Magnetic Motion Capture: Motion capture that is based on receivers that detect magnetic fields.

Magnetic Resonance Imaging (MRI): A way of making internal organs and structures visible by analyzing radio frequency emissions of atoms in a strong magnetic field. Can be made 3D by rendering large amounts of data.

Magneto-Optical Drives/Cartridges: These drives store data on removable, rewritable disc cartridges. When filled, a new cartridge is swapped for the old, eliminating the need to buy a new hard drive. Get LIM/DOW (Light Intensity Modulation/Direct Overwrite) disks/drive, which rewrites in one pass, resulting in 100% increase in write speed. Also known as MO.

Main Action Area: Area in the scene where most of the action takes place.

Mainframes: Early computer models whose components were housed in large steel frames.

Manual Focus: The digicam's focus can be set by the user at any point, from near to far; it is a useful override feature on some auto focus cameras, which sometimes refuse to fire when they cannot focus accurately in very low light or fast-moving subjects/objects.

Mapping a Sequence of Images: Mapping that is done by assigning 2D picture files that are applied as maps to 3D objects.

Markup: The instructions embedded in a text document that specify formatting features, such as headings and paragraphs.

Marquee: A large tent or a sizable and movable frame that identifies a selected portion of a bit-mapped image. It can be rectangular in shape or, in some cases, irregular.

Mask: An image that masks or protects a surface, or portions of it.

Mass: Measurement that equals density multiplied by volume.

Massively Parallel Computer: A computer that deals with very complex processing challenges by dividing up the tasks among a large number of small microprocessors.

Master: The original recorded copy or clone.

Master Background: A background exactly matching the cel set upon it.

Master Movie: When referring to QuickTime alternate movies, the master movie contains the display criteria for the other alternates as well as containing the fallback. It is the one to be embedded in a Web page.

Masthead: A graphic image placed on top of a Web page that tells end-users what page they are on. Masthead images can contain photos, text, shapes, and/or image maps.

Matchbands: An optical illusion caused by a sudden change in the rate of change of the brightness (discontinuities in the brightness' second derivative). This can give the appearance of a light or dark line at the sudden change.

Matching Background: See Key Master Background.

Matchmoving: The creation of a 3D computer graphic environment and camera to match live action and computer graphic components in a scene.

Material: The attributes describing how an object behaves and looks when lit.

Matte: A black, opaque silhouette that prevents exposure for a specific area of the film.

Matte Board: The easel on which artwork is mounted during the laboratory stage of matte photography.

Matte Line: The outline of an image caused from a less-than-perfect line-up between a matte and its corresponding image.

Matte Painting: A photo-realistic background composite with a live-action foreground.

Matte Photography: The art of photographing matte paintings in order to combine them with other components to create a composite.

Matting Technique: A technique that controls the degree of blending using different parts or aspects of the image map as a mask.

Maximum Aperture: A measure of how much light can pass through a lens when its diaphragm is fully opened. Lenses with maximum apertures of f-2 or f-2.8 are categorized as "fast" and can produce better exposures under lower light than "slow" lenses with maximum apertures of f-3.5 or smaller.

MCI (Media Control Interface): A multimedia commands/calls comprising Windows API (Application Program Interface).

Mean Filter: A filter that replaces a pixel with the average value of its surrounding pixels. It effectively blurs an image.

Measurements: Width preceding height given in inches. Character measurements are from the highest to the lowest point on the image.

Mechanical Effects: These are man-made effects that are achieved by built machines that are incorporated into a film. The sharks built for Jaws are examples of mechanical effects. Also referred to as Physical effects or Practical effects.

Media: The plural form of "medium"; anything that is used for storage or transmission of information such as disks or networks.

Media Control Interface: See MCI.

Median Filter: A filter that replaces a pixel with the "most typical" value of its surroundings while ignoring extreme values. It tends to remove "stray pixels" and small details.

Medium: In a digital context, the substance or object on which information is stored and transmitted.

Medium Close Up (MCU): A shot between a MS and a CU. (i.e., a human figure taken from the chest up).

Medium Long Shot (MLS): A shot that features topography and the sky, the ambient lighting, the weather and the time of day.

Medium Shot (MS): A camera angle often used to describe a shot of character from the waist up.

Megahertz: See Mhz.

MegaPixel: See MP.

Memory: The place that data is recorded and stored, either permanently or temporarily.

Memory Card Reader: A device that allows rapid transfer of images, recorded on digicam memory cards, to a computer. The memory card—containing a folder of images—shows up as an external drive on the computer's desktop. The entire folder can be copied to the hard drive in seconds.

MemoryStick: Sony's proprietary memory card.

Menu: A list of options from which users can choose, often available from a drop-down menu bar at the top of a graphical user interface (GUI).

Menu-Driven: A term that describes a type of interface that allows users to navigate by selecting choices from a menu of options on the screen, rather than typing characters on the command line.

Merchandising Artwork & Book Illustrations: Artwork produced for use on licensed product packaging, educational filmstrips or publications—the quality of which can vary because they are rarely created by the same artists that worked on the films themselves. In general, this type of artwork is worth much less than publicity or production art.

Mesh: A collection of faces that describe any type of object. The faces are arranged to form the outside surface of that object. The mesh is usually depicted in wireframe mode, as this shows the faces and the outline, and is quickly rendered.

Metaball: A type of "equipotential surface" around a point. This term also means to specify a point, radius and "intensity" for each ball, then when balls come close, their shapes blend to form a smooth equipotential surface. Very useful for modeling shapes such as animals and humans and can be rendered by most raytracing packages (also "blobs," "soft spheres" or "fuzzy spheres").

Metamorphosis: A clay animation technique in which one character is transformed into another by gradually resculpting the figure.

Metaphysics: The philosophical study of basic concepts of existence such as epistemology, ontology, aesthetics, and the meaning and purpose of life.

Meta-Tag: HTML tags that can be used to identify the creator of a Web page, which HTML specifications a Web page follows, the keywords and description of the page, etc. Most commonly used in online marketing with keywords and description tags, which tell search engines that index meta-tags what description to use in search query results.

MHEG-5: An open hypermedia ISO standard for portable multimedia/hypermedia applications on low-cost platforms.

Mhz (Megahertz): In relation to computer processors, it refers to the number of MIPS (million instructions per second).

Micromoney: A proposed Web-payment scheme wherein funds are subtracted from a user's bank account when buying digital tokens. The user then spends this encrypted micromoney at participating Websites without a credit card transaction.

Microsurgery: A form of surgery that lends itself to robotics and VR.

Middle of Story: The part of the story that usually contains the moments in which the main characters confront the conflicts that lead to a resolution.

MIDI (Musical Instrument Digital Interface): System of communication between digital electronic instruments allowing synchronization and distribution of musical information.

MIME (Multipurpose Internet Mail Extensions): A specification originally used for non-ASCII e-mail messages enabling them to be sent via the Internet. Web browsers also support various MIME types, which enable the browsers and the installed plug-ins to handle non-HTML files, such as movies and audio.

Miniature: Mini models, objects and scenes that are built for the purpose of incorporating into a movie set. Cars, buildings, and people are popular examples of traditional miniatures.

Minicomputers: Term used in the early days to describe a smaller mover accessible version of the mainframe computer. A computer that are smaller and less expensive than mainframes, yet almost as powerful.

MIP Mapping: A technique using scaled down versions of a texture image, generated beforehand and stored in memory, then used in rendering a 3D scene to provide the best quality. This technique allows objects to look more detailed close-up by defining multiple texture maps.

Mirror Site: An FTP site on the Internet that contains the same information held by another site, so that demand on the original site is distributed.

Mirror Worlds: Bird's-eye-views of a VR in which the viewer also exists and can be seen.

Mix: A combination of multiple tracks creating a finished song that can be heard on a CD or album.

Mixer: A device that creates several different versions of the same song, depending on the volumes, tempos and effects chosen in the mix. The individual tracks are then combined into a final mix that usually has only two tracks (stereo).

MLS: See Medium Long Shot.

MMC (MultiMedia Command): Standardized access to common features of SCSI-3 devices.

MMX (Multimedia Extension): A multimedia accelerator in Intel's Pentium processors that speeds media and communications processing 40-60%. Standard Pentiums move 1 byte of data at a time into the CPU for processing.

In contrast, MMX Pentiums move 8 bytes, all processed simultaneously.

MOD, Amiga MOD: A music (rather than a sound) format similar to MIDI. MOD files store digitized information about the instruments and the notes played. Common MOD file extensions are .mod, .mtm, and .s3m.

Mode: A method of specifying how color information is to be interpreted. An image can be converted to a different image mode (RGB to Indexed Color, for example). A blending mode can be chosen for a tool or layer to control how it affects underlying pixels.

Model Cel: A cel created by a studio's Ink and Paint department for accurate referencing of the character's features and proportions, used extensively during production; often of superior quality when compared to regular production cels.

Model Sheet: A group of drawings displaying various views of a character, designed to show the animators and assistants how the character is constructed.

Modeling: The spatial description and computer placement of imaginary 3D objects, environments and scenes.

Modeling Effect: Effectively using light to create depth and dimension in subject matter.

Models: All objects used in a scene.

Modem: A modulator or demodulator; the hardware required to connect telephone lines to the computer; essential for dial-up connections to the Internet.

Moderated Discussion List/Newsgroup: The moderator is a person who categorizes the topics and selects posts; a moderation discussion list/newsgroup is a service in which the moderator organizes participants' comments or suggestions into topics or categories.

Moire Pattern: A pattern of overlapping or finely spaced parallel lines that appear to form flowing arching patterns.

Monitor: A picture tube or screen that can display video signals and/or computer graphics.

Monochrome: One color. This term refers to a b/w monitor, or a monitor that uses one foreground and one background color, such as black and green.

Monoscopic Omni-Orientational Display: See MOOD.

MOO (Mud Object-Oriented): A specific implementation of a Mud system developed by Stephen white; located in the public domain for free download and use.

MOOD: (Monoscopic Omni-Orientational Display): HMD, Goggles, HUD, LCD. See also HOOD.

Morgue: A collection of graphic material, classified by a large number of different subjects that might be useful to a layout and background artist.

Morphing: A 2D effect that transforms one image into another; to add effects, such as reverb, that transform the sound of MP3 file; a corruption of the word "metamorphosis."

MOS (Multi Object Spectroscopy): A location scene shot without a mic.

Mother: The metal disc produced from mirror images of the father disc in the replication process. Mothers are used to make stampers, often called sons.

Motion Along Paths: Curves or lines are defined as paths along which an object, such as a camera, moves. For example, a walk-through might have two paths: one for the camera to follow and one for the target to move along.

Motion Blur: When recording reality with a video or film camera, we observe that objects moving too fast in front of the camera appear blurred.

Motion Capture: Allows the animator to capture live motion with the aid of a machine, and then apply it to computer-animated characters. It provides the kinematic information to the software by recording the positions or angles of live actors', or objects', joints in motion and uses sensors to detect movement in 2D or 3D space then record movements that can be applied to 3D animation.

Motion Choreography: In animation and computer graphics, the process of determining the displacement of each object over time.

Motion Compensation: A video-compression scheme used in MPEG.

Motion Constraints: Constraints imposed by rotation ranges.

Motion Control Photography: A photographic system in which a camera is connected to a computer-controlled apparatus.

Motion Control: Similar to motion capture, but is a two-way system—data can be output from computer software to hardware devices.

Motion Dynamics: Control the motion of 3D objects by applying forces to the joints and actually simulating the motion that would result in the physical world if such forces were applied to a real object with specific characteristics.

Motion Hold: When a character interrupts or concludes one motion and pauses.

Motion Parallax: Objects at different distances and fixation points move different amounts when the viewpoint is dollied along the X-axis (horizontal).

Motion Paths: Paths that provide an additional method of defining the motion of objects in 3D space.

Motion Platform: A controlled system that provides real motion to simulate the displayed motion in VR.

Motion Tests: Tests produced to preview the computer-animation sequences before final production.

Motion Tracking: Various methods of tracking camera motion without motion control. Motion-tracking data enables the recreation of an identical camera movement in a CGI element for compositing with the live-action scene.

Motivation: A psychological need, drive or feeling that raises the intensity of an action.

Mouse: An input device used to move a cursor and select files on the computer screen.

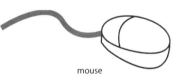

mouse

Mouseover: A popular special effect for Web graphics, generally programmed in Javascript, that changes color of a graphic image when cursor is placed over it; can also be used to trigger navigational changes and pop-up windows.

Mouth Action: The numerous shapes the mouth must make when speaking.

Moving Picture Experts Group: See MPEG.

Moving Water: A technique that can be recreated by placing spotlights (with varying cone angles) to shine up through a surface that represents water and has and animated shape.

Moviola: A trademarked name for a machine with a small rear-projection screen and the capacity to playback several sound tracks; used to edit and review footage, and to synchronize or interlock picture and sound track.

MP (MegaPixel): One million pixels. This term refers to when the length times width of a digicam's pixel array reaches one million, its resolution is then described in MegaPixels. For example, 1,300,000 pixels equal 1.3 MegaPixels.

MP4: One of several related standards for storing audio and video; see also MPEG Audio.

MPC/MPC2/MPC3 (Multimedia PC): An industry standard for a "minimal" multimedia computer system.

MPEG (Moving Picture Experts Group): Often used to refer to the standard file format and set of compression algorithms jointly developed by the Moving Picture Experts Group to handle video and audio. The various forms of MPEG are used for a wide range of video and audio applications, from desktop computer presentations and games to consumer DVD-Video players and satellite video systems.

MPEG-1: A format that produces high-quality video and audio streams at approximately 2x CD-ROM data rates. Standard MPEG-1 is full-frame rate (24: 30 fps, depending on the source) with a quarter-size image (352x240), and is useful for playback on most new desktop computers.

MPEG-2: A format that produces high data rate, full-broadcast-quality files. It requires an extremely fast computer and video card, or a hardware accelerator card;

the format for DVD-Video and many home satellite dish systems. Standard MPEG-2 is full-frame rate (24: 30 fps) and full-screen resolution (720x480).

MPEG Layer-2 Audio: Generally used for high-bandwidth MPEG audio at near CD quality; used for audio with both MPEG-1 and MPEG-2. Also known as MP2.

MPEG Layer-3 Audio: MPEG audio format popular on the Internet. It is generally used in audio-only files (.mp3 files), a lower-bandwidth format than MPEG Layer-2 audio, but still not ideal for modem streaming. Also known as MP3.

MPEG Video Format: MPEG (Moving Picture Experts Group) is the standard format for nearly all forms of digital video.

MRI: See Magnetic Resonance Imaging.

MS: See Medium Shot.

MTM: See Multitracker Music.

MUD (Multi-User Dungeon/Multi-User Dimension): Cyberspace in which users can take on an identity in the form of an avatar and interact with one another. Originally, MUDs tended to be adventure games played within enormous old castles with hidden rooms, trapdoors, exotic beasts, and magical items. Nowadays, the term is used more generically to refer to any cyberspace. Also known as 3D Worlds and Chat Worlds.

Mud Object-Oriented: See MOO.

Mu-Law: The digital encoding of voice based on pulse code modulation.

Multi Object Spectroscopy: See MOS.

Multicast: Transmitting the same media stream simultaneously to many recipients; delivery is similar to traditional television broadcast, in the sense that a stream is made available at a given time, and viewers may watch the part of that stream currently playing. Multicast delivery results in less network traffic than Unicast delivery because the signal is sent once.

MultiMedia Command: See MMC.

Multimedia Extension: See MMX.

Multimedia Kit: A package of hardware and software that adds multimedia capabilities to a computer; typically includes a CD-ROM or DVD player, a sound card, speakers, and a bundle of CD-ROMs.

Multimedia: The use of computers to present integrated text, graphics, video, animation, and sound.

Multimedia PC: See MPC/MPC2/MPC3.

Multimedia Speakers: A growing selection of high-quality computer speaker sets.

Multi-Pass Rendering: A technique used to separate different surface shading characteristics into separately rendered elements.

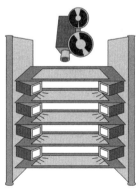

Multi-Person Space: Multiplayer space involving two or more human players. It's a type of interactive simulation giving users a sense physical virtual space.

multi-plane camera

Multi-Plane Camera: A special animation camera stand where elements were separated into different levels (backgrounds and foregrounds) painted on glass. During filming these elements were moved independently to give the illusion of depth and perspective.

Multi-Player Space: Cyberspace that emerges from simulation and is generated simultaneously by two or more decks.

Multiplexing: The process of combining audio and video data in a final MPEG file. See also Interleaving.

Multipurpose Internet Mail Extensions: See MIME.

Multi-Session: A CD-ROM drive that can read updated/changed CDs. Multi-session CD-ROM drives begin searching for directories by reading from the outside in, thus finding the furthermost directory. Single-session CD-ROM drives begin searching for directories from the inside out, thus only the first directory nearest the hub would be encountered.

Multi-Session CD-ROM: A CD-ROM technology that allows CD-ROMs to be recorded during multiple sessions or at different times.

Multi-Thread: A term that describes a program that is designed to have parts of its code executed concurrently.

Multi-Tracker Music (MTM): A type of MOD file.

Multi-User Dungeon/Multi-User Dimension: See MUD.

Multi-User Shared Hallucination: See MUSH.

MUSH (Multi-User Shared Hallucination): A text-based MUD system.

Music Archive Site: A Website or FTP site with MP3 files available to download.

Music Editor: An editor whose specialty is editing music tracks.

Music Montage: A series of scenes without dialog wherein music plays over the images. Often used to illustrate time passing, characters falling in love, etc.

Musical Instrument Digital Interface: See MIDI.

N

Nanomanipulation: The ability to visualize and affect objects in the nanometer range.

Narration: An audio commentary or voice-over that is frequently used in multimedia productions to provide spoken instructions, explain concepts, and "host" interactive programs.

National Television System Committee (NTSC): The television standard in the United States, Canada and Japan, which consists of 525 lines of resolution in each video frame. Each video frame consists of two fields, one with all the odd lines and the other with even lines, which are interlaced in one frame.

Native File Format: A custom file format to a specific program.

Native Signal Processing: A type of computing in which a powerful microprocessor performs the work of a digital signal processor (DSP) chip in realtime, allowing activities, such as video decoding, to be integrated with other functions in a single processing system.

Natural Phenomena: Affects based on nature.

Navigation: A term used to describe how a user moves through the structure of a new-media presentation.

Navigation Systems: Aids to navigation such as menus.

Near Clipping Plane: The visible area closest to the camera. Also known as Hither Plane.

Negative Matcher: An editor who specializes in assembling a negative reel by matching the scenes with the shots in the work reel.

Neon Glow: A type of glow on a graphic image that gives the appearance of neon lighting.

NET (No Electronic Theft): The law that makes it a felony to create or distribute unauthorized digital music.

Netiquette: Acceptable, proper behavior on the Internet; it applies primarily to e-mail and newsgroup posts.

Network Computer: An inexpensive PC "box" used with a television monitor, which is dedicated for use with the Internet.

Network Servers: Servers whose main purpose is to assist other computers on the functionality of a network to send and retrieve data.

Neural Interface: A version of the ultimate interface that connects VR directly to a human brain or nervous system.

Neuristic Listening: An alternate name for "psychoacoustics."

New Media: Media that have arisen since the 1970s.

Newbie: A person who is new to the Web, a newsgroup or e-mail, or any other application.

Newsgroups: Similar to large cork bulletin boards on which to post messages (known in newsgroup parlance as articles), ask questions, and get files. Also known as Usnet Groups.

Newsreader: A program with which to read newsgroups and post articles to them.

NiMH (Nickel Metal Hydride): A type of digicam rechargeable battery that provides very consistent voltage and is environmentally safe.

Nitrate Cels: Animation cels made from cellulose nitrate, a flammable, unstable material prone to wrinkling, yellowing and shrinking over long periods of time. Decomposing nitrate emits fumes and resins, which can accelerate the rate of decomposition of any cel in close proximity. Nitrate cel stock was used throughout the '20s, '30s and the early 40s at the Disney Studios, and well into the 50s at other studios.

Nitrate: See Cellulose Nitrate.

No Outlet: The scene (street) in which the driver must make a choice that implies severe consequences; no going back; the road of no return.

Nodal Point: A term that refers to where the focal point of a camera lens meets the film plane.

Nodal Point Offset: The distance between nodal point and actual point of rotation.

Noise Filter: An image filter that adds random pixels to an image to simulate a grainy appearance.

Noise: Anything that obscures a signal.

Noise Reduction: The process of removing unwanted noise from a signal; video: accomplished with filters such as blur, mean, or median. Uniform noise reduction applies one filter equally to each pixel. Adaptive noise reduction applies different filters to different types of noise.

Non-Disclosure Agreement: A common legal instrument used to stop contractors from sharing confidential information with competitors, or from making public any information addressed after the agreement.

Non-Interlaced: The video signal created when frames or images are rendered from a graphics program. Each frame contains a single field of lines being drawn one after another. See also Interlaced.

Nonlinear Editing (NLE): Editing performed on a computer, in which shots do not have to be placed one after the other (i.e., in a linear fashion).

Nonlinear Editor: An editing system based on storage of video and audio on computer disk, where the order or lengths of scenes can be changed without the necessity of re-assembling or copying the program.

Nonlinear: In the field of digital media: files or events that are indexed may be accessed immediately by users.

Non-Proportional Scaling: The process of resizing an object by different factors along each axis.

Non-Rational Curve: All control vertices on a spline having the same weight factor.

Non-Uniform Rational B-Spline (NURBS): A term meaning: Does not pass through its control points.

Normal Vector: A vector pointing straight out from (at right angles to) a surface.

Normalizing: The process of setting various frequency ranges to make the tracks sound more normal.

Not: A difference operator.

NTSC: See National Television System Committee.

Null Modem Cable: A RE-232-C cable wired in such a way that two computers can be connected and communicate without a modem.

Null Parent: A node in the hierarchy that does not relate to any specific part in the model, but controls several child objects together.

Number of Motion Sensors: Sensors used in motion capture gear.

NURBS: See Non-Uniform Rational B-Spline.

Nybble: Four bits, or half of one byte.

Nyquist Frequency: In digitizing audio, a sample rate equal to twice the speed of the highest frequency component in the content being sampled, including harmonics.

0

Object: In programming, a corporal body or abstraction with well-defined constituents and interpretations.

Object Animation: An animation technique, similar to puppet animation, in which objects appear to move by slight manipulation before each exposure.

Object Linking and Embedding: See OLE.

Object Space: A method for hidden surface removal making calculations in three dimensions.

Object/Local Coordinate System: Values relative to the origin of the object, which is sometimes placed in the center.

Object-Oriented: A programming technique that focuses design on the data (objects) and on the user interfaces. Object-oriented design is also the mechanism for defining how modules "plug and play."

Oblique Scene: A scene that is unexpected, surprising to the audience and/or a character.

Obstruction of Light: Light effect caused by objects, such as dry leaves, being swept in front of the light source.

Occipital Cortex: The back of the brain receiving retinotopic projections of visual displays.

Occlusion: The effect of one 3D object blocking another object from view.

OCR: Optical Character Recognition.

Octahedron: An eight-sided rectangular polyhedral.

Offline: A term that describes an operation that occurs independently and is not under the control of a computer.

OLE (Object Linking and Embedding): A Windows' method of transferring objects from one program to another; the process involves copying and pasting using the clipboard. Paste Linking (available as a Paste Special option), plants a trail to return to the original/source document so that when the original changes, they are visible in the receiver. Paste Embedding, the default paste mode, places a copy of the original into the receiver. Because the two programs are not linked, any changes to the original are not reflected in the receiver.

On Ones, Twos, or Threes: Terms that refer to the number of frames where each drawing is held during filming. The smoothest animation is done on ones and twos, which means 12 or 24 drawings are used per second of screen time.

On Ramp: The last street or scene in Act One of a 22-minute formatted script; includes the story signposts, and is the first act out.

On-Demand: Video that is not broadcasted live—it is filmed, but compressed and made available on a server.

One of One: A premium production drawing, usually framed side-by-side with a matching hand-painted, one-of-a-kind cel created from that drawing. Many one-of-one presentations feature characters and qualities virtually impossible to find in any form other than limited editions. The one-of-one cel is usually numbered "1/1."

Onionskin: A term that originated from traditional cel animation. It's a technique that by drawing on a translucent medium, with a light source beneath the drawing surface, an animator can see the position of an object on one page, while drawing it in a new position on the page above.

Online: A term that refers to being connected to the Internet. Online advertising is done exclusively on the Web or via e-mail.

Online Marketing: Advertising that is done exclusively on the Web or via e-mail. Various types of online marketing include: Affiliate programs; search engine optimization; banner advertising, directory enhancement; posts to moderated discussion lists; newsgroups and forums; e-mail advertising and online press releases.

Online Service: A business providing a wide variety of data transmitted via phone lines to subscribers, often with an infrastructure allowing subscribers to communicate with one another and connect with a variety of third-party information providers.

Online/Offline Editing: Offline editing is the less expensive creative process of putting together an Edit Decision List (EDL). Online editing uses more expensive equipment to assemble the final product based on the EDL, and can utilize special effects equipment.

Ontology: The metaphysics of existence.

Opacity: A compliment of transparency; the measurement of an object's ability to block light transmission.

Opaquing: Cel painting. A painter is referred to as an Opaquer.

Open Architecture: A term related to microcomputers, a hardware configuration that allows the addition of circuit boards, which are typically plugged into slots on a motherboard to expand the functionality of the original system.

OpenGL: A 3D graphics procedural interface developed by Silicon Graphics, Inc., based on their earlier proprietary GL graphics library.

Optical Character Recognition: See OCR.

Optical Effects: See Visual Effects.

Optical Motion Capture: To utilize lights, cameras, and reflective dots to determine the position of the joints in 3D space.

Optical Printer: A machine used to combine live action and animation, as well as other special effects.

Optical Resolution: The highest resolution that a scanner can capture without interpolation.

Opticals: A composite created by the use of an optical printer, which takes one or more film elements, aligns them and photographs them onto a new piece of film.

Optical Viewfinder: An optical glass device on the digicam that, when looked through, shows the intended image to be photographed. Some digicams have optical viewfinders in addition to LCD monitors because the LCD can "wash out" in bright sunlight, making it virtually impossible to see the image.

Optical Zoom: A zoom lens that uses movement of lens elements to achieve various fields of view. Regardless of the zoom settings, the resolution of the image remains the same.

Opt-In: An e-mail marketing term in which the recipient specifically requests e-mail related to a specific topic of interest.

Orange Book: The standard for WORM (Write Once Read Many) CDs; used to archive/back up catalogs, directories, and other computerized paperwork.

Orientation: A term that includes tilt, roll, and pan.

Origin: The main point of reference.

Original: The film on which a picture was originally shot.

Orthogonal: The most common type of parallel projection. Also known as Flat Projection.

Orthographic Projection: The visible outline of an object projected to a surface on which the projection vector is parallel to the Z-axis (depth).

Outline: In graphic design, a term that refers to the tracing of the outer edge of text or a graphic image.

Output Movie: Compressed video ready for playback and distribution.

Output: To send data from a computer or processor to another device, such as a printer or disk drive.

Outsource: To hire a specialist, consultant, or an external production company to produce segments of media types.

Overall Blending: A process that controls the degree by which the image map blends uniformly with all the attributes of the surface.

Overhead Light: Lighting that creates a dramatic halo around the top of the subject.

Overlapping Motion: A term that refers to when some motions start before others conclude.

Overlay: Foreground elements of the setting are painted on a cel and placed over the characters to give the illusion of depth.

Overlay Where Not Zero: An image compositing method in which the overlay image results wherever it is not zero, and the background image results wherever the overlay image is zero. It's a rather simplistic method, but is sometimes supported in low-end hardware and can be useful in overlaying text, for example.

Overmodeling: Creating too many elements.

Oversampling: To read data at a higher rate than normal to produce more accurate results, or to make it easier to sample.

Overscan: A condition in which a video signal bleeds off the edges of a monitor.

P

Paint Palette: An electronic version of an artist palette allowing the user to select from a wide variety of colors or mix to create new colors.

Paint Pots: Controls that adjust video color.

Paintbrush: A tool that simulates painting with a paintbrush.

Painter: The person responsible for coloring the inked drawings on a cel with paint.

Painting Tool: A command or function of an image-editing program that simulates traditional art or photographic tools.

PAL (Phase Alternate Line): The European color TV broadcasting standard featuring 625 lines per frame and 25 frames per second. See NTSC and SECAM.

Palette: A selection of colors available in a graphics application.

Palette Image Format: A format used to store images that works much like pseudo color in a display controller. Each pixel contains a color ID instead of the actual color value. The true color represented by each color ID is defined in a table called the palette, which must also be stored with the image.

Palletized Texture: Compressed texture formats, such as 1-, 2-, 4-, and 8-bit instead of 24-bit, allowing more textures to be stored in less memory.

Pan (Cinemascope): A cel or drawing as large as 12"x30"; used in such classics as Lady and the Tramp and Sleeping Beauty.

Pan: A technique in which artwork is moved under the camera to give the effect of the camera following the action, or scanning a scene.

Pan (Yaw): A rotation around its Y-axis (vertical).

Pan and Scan: A dynamic cropping technique used to translate between materials with different aspect ratios; often used to translate movies shot on wide-screen film formats to 4:3 television display. In the pan and scan process, the image is cropped to the new aspect ratio, and the transfer operator pans within the wider original image to include important details which are near the edge. Movies that have been "pan and scanned" do not have any black bars (letterboxing) and completely fill the television screen.

Pan Cel: A cel or set-up wider than standard, used for moving (panning) camera shots.

Pan Chart: The charted camera calibrations affixed to the top of the artwork for a pan.

Pan Shot: A term derived from "panoramic," that refers to a shot that encompasses a wider area than can be viewed by the camera at one time, which will be scanned by the camera via panning.

Panning Peg Bars: Specialized moveable pegs on the compound, calibrated and controlled by dials, which allow the artwork to be moved to accommodate moving shots, such as pans. Also known as Traveling Peg Bars.

Panning Shots: See Pan Shot.

Pantone Matching System: See PMS.

Parallel Action: A term that refers to when the audience is shown actions that take place at the same time, in different locations.

Parallel Plotting: A term that refers to when the subplot parallels the main plot, telling the same story from another character's point of view.

Parameter Curve: A graph representing curved interpolations.

Parameter Space: Space used to position image maps on curved patches.

Parametric Animation: An animation control method in which the scene state is determined by mathematical functions or computer procedures that use animation time as an input parameter.

Parametric Curved Surface: Mathematically defined freeform curves.

Parametric Motion Control: A technique used to animate complex mechanical parts and assemblies—when an element becomes an actor, the way it moves (position and orientation) is defined as a function of time.

Parents: Object(s) at the top of the hierarchy.

Parietal Cortex: An area of the brain adjacent and above the occipital cortex thought to process spatial location and direction.

Parody: A comical or satirical imitation of a person or thing. A film that makes fun of another film's plot or characters.

Particle Systems: A system based on employing simple shapes in 3D space. These are software systems that enable the operator to create natural phenomena, such as rain, snow, and water that are based on collections of particles that exhibit behavior rather then geometric shapes.

Path of Action: The movement of a character throughout a scene; used in layout.

Path: A sequence of points used to draw images consisting of line segments.

Payoff: The reward resulting from watching a film or animation. For example, the director may create an extremely funny end to the film to payoff the audience for watching the film— the absence of a payoff may leave the audience feeling cheated, as there was no point to the film.

PC Paintbrush Format: A graphics file format that stores raster graphics.

PCD: The Photo CD format; the graphics file format that Kodak uses to store images on Photo CD.

PCI (Peripheral Component Interface): A very fast I/O bus (with potential of 132 MBps transfer rate).

PCMCIA: Personal Computer Memory Card International Association.

PCX: The graphics file format, created by ZSoft's PC PaintBrush program that stores raster graphics images.

PDA (Portable Digital Assistant): A personal and portable palm held device that can preform such basic functions as scheduling to complex functions that are equal to that of a personal desktop computer.

PDA

PDF (Portable Document Format): Created by Adobe Systems Inc. as a universal browser; files can be downloaded via the Web and viewed page-by-page, provided the user's computer has installed the necessary plug-in, which can be downloaded from Adobe's Website.

Peg Holes: The holes on animation paper and cels that fit over pegs on animation discs and camera stands; by aligning the pegs and holes, the cels and backgrounds remain in proper positioning.

Pegs: Small metal or plastic projections affixed to all surfaces that will support the artwork during production; used to maintain registration through all stages of production by fitting into corresponding holes. Also known as Peg Bars.

Pencil Drawing: The original drawings created by the film's animators from which the cels are traced or Xeroxed onto a cel. Also known as Animation Drawing.

Pencil Model Sheet: A group of original pencil drawings on one sheet that illustrate an animated character in a variety of poses and expressions. May consist of several final drawings cut from other paper and mounted together on a new sheet; final model sheets are then lithographed and distributed to the animation team to ensure a uniform look and feel to a character throughout a production.

Pencil Test: A film or videotape of the animator's pencil drawing used during production to check the timing and smoothness of the animation.

Pencil Tool: A software "painting" tool that simulates drawing with a pencil.

Penumbra: The area in the edges of the shadow that blends with other lights in the environment.

Performance Animation: Character animation using data input from motion-capture or real-time puppet devices.

Peripheral Component Interface: See PCI.

Peripheral Storage: The storage based on the volume, quality, and complexity of the work done at the computer animation facility.

Persistence of Vision: The property of the human visual system to continue seeing an image a short time (fraction of a second) after it has disappeared.

Perspective Correction: A method of texture mapping, extremely important for creating a realistic image, that takes into account the effect of the Z value in a scene, while mapping texels (texture elements) onto the surface of polygons. As a 3D object moves away from the viewer, the length and height of the object become compressed, making it appear shorter.

Perspective Point: Usually on the horizon, a point in the picture upon which objects fall into the background.

Perspective Projection: Projection that projects all objects in the 3D environment onto the image plane.

Perspective: The rules that determine the relative size of objects on a flat page to give the impression of 3D distance.

P-Frame (Predictive Frame): MPEG difference frame that looks to previous frames; similar to a QuickTime/AVI delta frame.

Phase Alternate Line: See PAL.

Phenakistiscope: An early-animation device that uses a disc with sequential drawing around its border in front of a mirror to create the illusion of motion.

Phong Lighting: A method of lighting a 3D world, the Phong lighting model applies three types of lighting to the vertex of each polygon; performs operations based on the normal of the polygon, the "normal" being an imaginary line drawn orthogonal (straight up from) the face of the polygon.

Phong Render: A process that mimics the effect of ray tracing, without use of its mathematical processes, to produce an image without reflections.

Phong Shading: A 3D surface shading method, developed by Phong Bui-Toung, which interpolates the colors over a polygonal surface, giving accurate reflective highlights and shading.

Photographic Lines: The Disney Studios developed a method of reproducing animation drawings to cel by means of a photographic process—in scenes that the camera was to be tightly focused on a small character, this process would produce a hairline more accurate than could be achieved by hand inking. The animation was rendered at full size and would be reduced photographically to fit the scene. The photographic lines could be dyed several colors, but close up they sometimes appeared to be slightly translucent. This technique was discontinued after the development of xerography.

Photokinestasis: An illusion of movement is achieved by moving static artwork, usually photographs, collages, or reproductions of paintings, under the camera.

Photo-Multiplier: A very sensitive vacuum tube that detects light and converts it to electrical signals.

Photorealism: A computer graphics image that is not distinguishable from reality.

Photoshop: A popular 2D software application created by Adobe Systems for the purpose of manipulating images, painting and drawing. Photoshop is available on both Macintosh and PC platforms.

Physical Effects: See Mechanical Effects.

PICS: A file format deriving its name from the word "pictures"; convenient when a series of images is required for animation purposes.

PICT: A still image file format developed by Apple Computer, PICT files can contain vector and bitmap images, as well as text and an alpha channel. It's a ubiquitous image format on MacOS.

Pictogram: A visual representation of a word or object.

Picture CD: Similar to Photo CD, but with only one medium resolution scan for each image.

Picture Files: Rendered images.

Picture Maps: A color map.

Pinch Filter: A special effects filter that squeezes the center of an image creating a pinched look.

Pipeline: The process used to create computer-generated images.

Piracy: The unauthorized and illegal duplication or distribution of copyrighted material.

Pit Stop Principle: The process of taking several days or weeks off to refuel your imagination, therefore returning to the script with fresh energy.

Pitch: To tell a story idea to editors as succinctly and enthusiastically as possible, capturing the tone of their cartoon series.

Pixel: A picture element that corresponds to a small piece of computer memory; a single unit of a digital image in print or on a CRT monitor such as a television or computer; sometimes referred to as dots—as in dots per inch. This term may also describe the collection of digital information elements that are specific to a single spatial sampling site in an image—for example, three-color component samples and a transparency-component sample.

Pixel Aspect Ratio: The shape of the individual pixels in a raster image.

Pixel Clock: A clock used to divide the horizontal line of video into samples. Must be stable (a very small amount of jitter) relatively to the video, to avoid improper image storage. The higher the frequency of the pixel clock, the more samples per line.

Pixelation: A stop-motion technique in which full-sized props and live actors are photographed frame-by-frame to achieve unusual effects of motion.

Pixellization: when the pixels making up a digital image are so large that they are visible causing a mosaic effect that is know as pixellization.

Pixmap: A raster image file with more than 8 bits per pixel.

Placement of Sensors: This placement depends on the number of sensors available, the types of motion-sensor technology being used, the type of motion that is being captured, the type of data being sent to the computer-animation program, and the type of motion constraints implemented into the computer-animation program.

Plates: A reel of motion picture film that serves as the background image when a composite of any kind is being assembled.

Platen: A sheet of heavy glass used to hold cels flat and motionless during shooting.

Platform: A particular hardware and software operating system, such as IBM-compatible/DOS platform, or the Macintosh platform.

Player: A type of software that plays MP3 or other audio files.

Playlist: A list of MP3 files to be played in a specified order.

Playlist Editor: Software designed to create playlists.

Plenoptic Images: The "plenoptic function" of Adelson and Bergen is a parameterized function used to describe everything that is visible from a given point in space. McMillan and Bishop provide a concise problem statement for image-based rendering paradigms, such as morphing and view interpolation.

Plot: The central idea of a story or movie.

Plotter: An output device similar to a printer that draws of plots a 2D image on paper.

Plug-In: A software extension that provides added capabilities to the browser, for purposes such as viewing, hearing or saving specially formatted files. Most plug-ins are available for download via the creator's Web page.

PMS: Pantone Matching System.

PNG (Portable Network Graphics Format): This format is used for lossless compression and displaying images on the Web. It is advantageous because it supports images with millions of colors and produces background transparency without jagged edges; disadvantageous because PNG images will not appear on older browsers, and are comparatively larger in file size than GIFs.

Point: Defined by its XYZ location.

Point Light Source: A source in which light is seen. Although real light becomes dimmer in distance, a computer graphics point light source may not work that way unless explicitly stated.

Point of Interest (POI): The center of interest; the focus of the camera.

Point of Light (POL): Casts light evenly in all directions.

Point of View (POV): The viewing point; the location of camera placement.

Point Primitive: A graphic primitive that is an area enclosed by a loop of straight edges. For example, triangles and squares are polygon primitives.

Point Size: The convention of measuring type fonts on screen; 72 points equals one inch.

Polygons: 2D, open contours are almost always built with polygonal or linear splines, and can be defined by a number of sides and radius. Polygons are three connected points in space connected by straight lines.

Polyline: A continuous line composed of one or more line segments. A polyline can be created by specifying the endpoints of each segment. When using draw programs, one can treat a polyline as a single object, or divide it into its component segments.

Pop: When an object's visible appearance suddenly changes, or an object appears out of nowhere; usually an undesired artifact of poor LOD.

Port: A point of I/O access to a computer or system; to convert a program on one platform to run on another. For example, from Unix to MS-DOS or MacOS).

Port Address: This term is used to ensure each server application responds only to requests and communications from appropriate clients, each server is assigned a port address. Also known as Port Number.

Portable: The ability to be exchanged between several programs.

Portable Document Format: See PDF.

Portable Network Graphics: See PNG.

Portals: Polygons that, once passed through, automatically load a new world or execute a user-defined function.

Portfolio: A collection of works/samples to display skills to potential clients or employers.

Pose-to-Pose Animation: A method in which the animator plans the movements in advance, enabling him to draw the extremes—the assistant animator then draws the in between.

Position Trigger: A hotspot, sensitive spot, or button that begins a computation when touched.

Post: Jargon for post-production—the part of a video or multimedia production performed in a studio after live filming. Post can also describe the construction of basic images.

Posterization: A process that significantly reduces the grayscale levels of an image.

Post-Production: The work done on a film upon photography completion, such as editing, developing, and printing.

PostScript: The page description language, created and licensed by Adobe Systems Inc., used to display and print fonts and images.

Potentiometers: Devices capable of measuring electromotive force based on the amount of energy that passes through the device as a result of the joint motion.

PPI (Pixels Per Inch): A term that specifies the resolution of an input device, such as a scanner, digital camera, or monitor. For example, Web page resolution ranges from 72-96 pixels per inch.

Practice: To perform or work at repeatedly so as to become proficient.

Preamp: A hardware or software device that sets the level of music before it is amplified. Hardware preamps are often used to boost and filter the signal of a turntable or cassette desk prior to the signal being amplified.

Predictive Encoding: In MPEG compression, the storage of differences between a prediction of the data, and the actual data in subsequent frames, which result in higher compression ratios.

Predictive Frame: See P-Frame.

Preferences File: The contents of this control the result of many operations, functions, and tools directly and indirectly.

Pre-Flash: Some digicams fire two flashes, the first pre-flash) adjusts the white balance, the second exposes the picture. It is different from red-eye reduction mode in

---

which multiple weak flashes are fired to close the subject's iris prior to the actual exposure.

Preliminary: Art used in the developmental stages of a film. Also known as Pre-Production.

Premise: The second phase in animation writing. It's a brief summary of a story, including all major plot points and action sequences. It should also include all characters in the story, and capture the tone of the cartoon in the most exciting way; considered to be the written sales pitch of the story idea, and is a few paragraphs to two pages in length.

Premium Channels: Program services purchased by cable subscribers for an extra fee. An all-movie channel such as HBO is an example of a premium channel.

Prepared Background: See Presentation Background.

Pre-Production: A process that involves all conceptualization and planning that takes place before a computer-animation project is produced.

Presence: A defining characteristic of a good VR system. It's a feeling of being there, immersed in the environment, able to interact with other objects.

Presentation Background: A background created by a specific studio for publicity or display purposes; created to enhance a cel's value and visual appeal; genre includes those backgrounds that a consumer might have specifically prepared for a particular cel.

Presentation Setups: When the contract with Courvoisier Galleries expired in 1946, the Disney Studios continued to assemble cel setups in nearly identical packaging to give to clients, VIPs and studio guests. Because the production cels were often imperfect, damaged or unavailable, these cel setups were created to order by the ink-and-paint department using poses taken from original animation drawings. These cels were usually combined with a production background, or a simple complementary painting created by the background department in downtime.

Presentation Software: Packages, such as Microsoft Powerpoint, which allow users to create "electronic overhead transparencies." Typically easy to use, presentation software has all the full multimedia capabilities found in authoring software.

Presentation Storyboard: A storyboard used to show a detailed visual summary of the project to decision-makers.

Pre-Visualization: The process of cobbling together a sequence or image to illustrate the final look of the project before it is actually finished. This can be computer-generated using 2D or 2D software programs, rendered in sketch format, or through the use of miniature models. Also known as Pre-Vis.

Primary Colors: A set of colors that can be combined to produce any desired set of intermediate colors, within a limitation call the "gamut". The primary colors for color television are red, green, and blue. The exact red, green, and blue colors used are dependent on the television standard.

Primary Motion: The motion that captures the audience's attention.

Primitives: Related to 2D graphics, these are simple shapes, such as squares, triangles and circles.

Printer Resolution: The number of dots per inch that a printer can print. The higher the dpi number (i.e.: 300 dots per inch), the better the image quality.

Printer: Computer peripherals for producing hard copy on paper and other similar media.

Procedural Creation: Creation that relies on mathematical functions or computer programs to create images that are usually abstract.

Procedural Description: Objects are modeled by simulating their natural growth process that is described in the form of procedures.

Procedural Model: An object model defined implicitly by a program that can produce volume or surface elements.

Procedural Motion: Animates the objects in the scene based on a set of procedures and rules to control motion.

Procedural Textures: The use of shaders or small pieces of programming code, to describe 3D surfaces, and lighting and atmosphere effects.

Process Color: The four colors used to print color—cyan, magenta, yellow, and black (CMYK). This term also describes the page description language, created and licensed by Adobe Systems Inc., used to display and print fonts and images.

Processing: The manipulation of data from one state to another, usually at the request of an operator or user.

Production: The original artwork used in the production of a film rather than for publicity or display. Also describes the process that involves a series of standard steps: modeling, animation, and rendering.

Production Backgrounds: Artwork over which a series of cels is photographed, including art from a particular sequence not used in the final film, or a portion edited from a finished sequence.

Production Cel: The final result of creating animation using traditional ink and paint techniques, designed for art which we see on the movie screen. Cel inkers transfer the animator's drawings onto transparent acetate sheets, and cel painters paint the character's colors on the reverse side. Each cel is then photographed against a background by a special movie film camera.

Production Cel & Background Setup: An original production cel combined with a production background used in the final version of an animated film or short. Typically, cels and backgrounds may be matched after the filmmaking process for aesthetic reasons.

Production Drawing: A term that describes the animator's drawings, which are used as the basis for creating animation cels.

Production Storyboard: The storyboard that guides the production of an animated project.

Production Team: A group of individuals who execute the idea provided by the creative team, then deliver the completed animation.

Professional Market: A group of customers who purchase software or production equipment for use on the job; the opposite of the consumer market.

Progressive Scan: A progressive scan display draws the lines of the screen in order from top to bottom. For example, computer displays.

Projected Reality: A VR system that uses projection screens rather than HMDs or personal display monitors. See Real Projection.

Projection Map: An image that is projected onto objects in a scene.

Projection Speed: The rate at which the moves through a projector; 24 frames is the standard for all sound films.

Promotional Cel: A non-production cel used for promotional purposes only; usually perfectly posed main characters. Also known as Publicity Cel.

Proportional Scaling: The resizing of an object along each axis in equal amounts.

Proprietary: A term that describes material, owned by an individual or an entity, not available for use without permission.

Props: Objects within the scene to be used by characters.

Prose: The description of a scene or action by grouping lines together.

Prosthetic Motion Capture: Motion capture that provides accurate angular rotation data and is based on potentiometers.

Protagonist: The main character of the story; the driver.

Pseudo Color System: A graphics system that stores pseudo colors, not true colors, in its bitmap. Pseudo colors are translated to true colors by the color lookup table (LUT).

Psychoacoustics: The study of determining what the human ear can hear.

Public Domain: Intellectual property that may be freely copied, performed and distributed. It happens when copyright expires, or by the declaration of the copyright owner(s) stating that the material is in the public domain.

Publicity & Promotional Artwork: See Publicity Cel and Promotional Cel.

Publicity Cel: Non-production cel created for promotional or publicity purposes.

Pun: The humorous use of a word in a way that suggests two or more interpretations; play on words.

Punch: The device that cuts registration holes in cels and drawing paper so they can be placed over the corresponding pegs.

punch device

Punch Filter: A special-effects filter that causes the image to appear as if the center has been expanded.

Puppet Animation: 3D articulated figures that are manipulated on miniature sets and photographed frame-by-frame.

Purging: A process used to automatically eliminate excessive vertices in complex 3D models.

Push Web Technology: This technology publishes/broadcasts personalized information to subscribers, then, rather than using bookmarks and search engines to pull down information, users run a client application updated with data that is "pushed" down by a server. Also known as Web-Casting or Channel-Casting.

Put Down: Name-calling and/or a type of insult.

Pyramid of Vision: The portion of the 3D environment that is seen through the camera. Also known as Cone of Vision.

Pyrotechnics: A branch of physical effects that deal with the controlled use of explosives and fires.

Q

Quad Chroma: A term that refers to a technique whereby the sample clock is four times the frequency of the color burst. For NTSC, this means that the sample clock is about 14.32 MHz (4 x 3.579545 MHz); for PAL the sample clock is about 17.73 MHz (4 x 4.43361875 MHz). These are popular sample clock frequencies because, depending on the method chosen, they make the chrominance (color) decoding and encoding easier.

Quad Mesh Primitive: A graphic primitive that contains a grid of quadrilaterals.

Query Letter: A written letter sent to acquire permission to submit a sample script that should include the point of the letter, information about the writer, a brief synopsis of the script, and any acclaim the script has garnered.

Query: A search request submitted to a database (such as the search engine and directory databases) to find a particular piece of information, or all records that meet the search criteria.

Quick Mask: In PhotoShop, a screen display mode in which a translucent colored mask covers selected or unselected areas of an image— painting tools can be used to reshape a Quick Mask.

QuickTime Movies: A video format used by Apple for multimedia files; the common extension is .mov.

QuickTime Video: The Apple technology that allows video, digitized sound and music, 3D, and virtual reality to be viewed on a Website; available for Macintosh- and Windows-based computers.

QuickTime/JPEG: A file format useful when saving both still images and animated sequences in a variety of levels of image compression and quality.

QuickTime/VR: An enhanced version of the QuickTime standard developed by Apple to display multimedia content (animation, audio and video) on computers, adding the ability to display and rotate objects in three dimensions. A QuickTime VR plug-in is available for most Web browsers.

R

Radio Button: In an online form, radio buttons (usually round graphic representations) are used to illustrate on or off, or selected or unselected.

Radio Frequency: Electromagnetic waves in the bandwidth between 10 kHz and 3 MHz propagated in the air without a guide wire or cable.

Radiosity: A diffuse illumination calculation system for graphics based on energy balancing that takes into account the multiple reflections off many walls or surfaces.

RAID (Redundant Array of Independent Disks): A group of disk drives with a controller creating a storage system that acts as one disk with higher performance than the individual drives.

RAM (Random Access Memory): The working memory of a computer storing programs and data so that the CPU can access them directly.

Random Distortion: A process that is useful in creating models of terrains with so many irregularities that it would be difficult to model them with other techniques.

Raster Graphics: Computer graphics whereby the images are stored as groups of pixels. A raster is an electron beam that sweeps in horizontal lines across the faceplate of a cathode ray tube "painting" images on the phospher-coated screen of a monitor.

Raster: The area illuminated by the scanning beam of a display grid.

Rasterization: The process of transforming a 3D image into a set of colored pixels.

Rate of Change: This term is defined by the necessary amount of time to get from one key frame to another, and by the amount of change in the animated parameters.

Rate of Display: The number of frames of animation per second.

Rational Curve: A term that refers to when the values of the weights on the curves are modified.

Raw Motion: Motion that contains too much noise and must be cleaned.

Raw Stock: Film that has not been exposed or processed.

Ray Casting: A term used to denote non-recursive raytracing.

Raytracing: A rendering system that traces the path of light from objects to light sources; See Backward Raytracing.

Raytracing Depth: A term related to the number of times that a ray will may come in contact with surfaces in the 3D space.

Read Only Memory (ROM): Usually stores programs vital to the operation of a personal computer, and can only be written once.

Readability of Motion: Results in flowing action, while confusing motion will result in unfocused action.

Real Projection: A VR projection system or a pun on "rear projection."

Real Time: Appearing to be without lag or flicker; for example, 60 cps displays. It's considered highly interactive computation.

Real Video: Software that delivers "broadcast-quality" video via the Internet in real time; operates with 28.8 Kbps— or higher—modems.

Real-Audio: A popular file format for sound created by RealNetworks. Files are compressed to minimize size, but are not as compressed as MP3 files.

Real-Audio Plugin: A helper application enabling viewers to listen to live AM-quality audio via the Web.

Real-Time Compression: The compression of movies as soon as they enter the computer. Also known as One-step Capture.

Real-Time Rendering: A term that refers to when the computer updates the screen with an actual rendered image rather than a mesh on the fly. This is most often done in flat rendering modes because the more complicated rendering modes, such as Phong or Gouraud, require more computer muscle and cannot render in real time. Real-time rendering makes virtual reality possible.

Real-Time Transfer Protocol: See RTP.

Receivers: Electronic devices that receive signals, transmit, or deliver by any means, and decode them.

Record: The output of an image to videotape or film.

Recording Mode: The method used to rip a file from a CD. Digital mode is up to five times faster that analog recording, and provides a slightly cleaner MP3 file. Analog mode "listens" to the CD as it plays then records. Analog recording will only move as fast as the CD plays in the drive.

Rectangular Coordinate System: A term that defines specific locations and accurately positions the points of objects in a 3D space.

Rectangular Polyhedral: Objects with multiple facets.

Red Book: An industry standard, defined by Philips and Sony, for CD audio and CD-ROM drives. This is one of the levels of standards, which are traditionally referred to by the color of the cover in which the documents were originally bound, is the Red Book, which is most frequently used with respect to end-user CD audio and CD-ROM drives. Also specifies the standards for the recording and playback media.

Red-Eye: A phenomenon that occurs when a flash is fired directly into the subject's eyes within a dim or dark environment—blood vessels in the back of the eye reflect their color back through the iris of the eye which is usually widely opened.

Redundant Array of Independent Disks: See RAID.

Reflection Map: A map that consists of a 2D that is applied to a 3D surface with the purpose of making the surface reflective.

Reflection Rays: Rays that travel straight through the scene and bounce off the reflective surfaces; refers to when the ray-tracing process encounters transparent surfaces in the scene.

Reflection Vector: A vector used in the Phong lighting model to compute the specular reflection—the points in the direction from which light is reflecting off the object.

Reflective Color: The color perceived from reflected light off a surface.

Reflectivity: A surface's ability to reflect the surrounding world.

Reflex Viewing: The intended image viewed directly by your eye. Also known as TTL (through the lens) and SLR (single lens reflex) viewing.

Refraction: The bending of light when passing between mediums.

Refresh Rate: The rate at which parts of the image on a CRT are repainted or refreshed. The horizontal refresh rate is the rate at which individual scan lines are drawn. The vertical refresh rate is the rate at which fields are drawn in interlaced mode, or whole frames are drawn in non-interlaced mode.

Registered: A term that refers to the portion of a character on a cel that appears incomplete or cut off because it has been drawn to align with the background, foreground or other elements.

Registration: The exact alignment of the various pieces of artwork in relation to each other using the peg system.

Re-Issue Courvoisier: S/R labs can re-issue all Courvoisier seals, stamps, and certificates for art originally released through the Courvoisier program. See also Courvoisier.

Release Print: An additional print made after an approved answer print, incorporating the same corrections. Also known as Composite Print.

Remix: To create different versions of a song using the same tracks.

Remote Rendering: A term that refers to when the rendering of a 3D model takes place in one of the other machines on the network.

Renaissance: A period of art dominated by the exploration of perspective.

Render: To create a new image based on a transformation of an existing image or 3D scene.

Rendering: The process of generating the final image in the computer, which takes the modeling, animation, lighting, texture and color data, and decides the color of each pixel per frame.

Renderman: The Renderman standard describes necessary computer knowledge before rendering a 3D scene, such as the objects, light sources, cameras, and atmospheric effects.

Rending Farm: Many computers solely dedicated to network rendering.

Replacement Animation: The technique in which multiple sculptures are produced and brought to life by shooting each for one frame.

Reproduction Backgrounds: Backgrounds created using various techniques including photography, xerography, and lithography.

Reproduction Cel: See Limited Edition Cel.

Resample: To change the resolution of an image; resampling down discards pixel information in an image, while resampling up adds pixel information through interpolation.

Resizing: To change an image size, by squeezing pixels together or spreading them apart, without changing the image's file size. See also Interpolation.

Resolution: A measure of an object's dpi.

Resolution Independence: A term used to describe equipment, such as computers, that can operate at more than one resolution.

Rest Area: A scene in which the character and/or audience can take a rest from the tension of the plot; serves as an emotional or comical moment for a character.

Retrace: The return of the electron beam (inside a computer display) to the upper-left corner, after making one pass.

Reverberation: The simulation of natural reverberation (such as the echoing caused by sound reflection), in order to add a sense of spaciousness and ambience to a sound.

Reverse Cropping: The process of artificially extending the boundaries of an image to obtain more space by duplicating existing elements in the image.

RGB (Red, Green, Blue): Web colors are defined in terms of a combination of these three colors. For example, conversely, print designers typically define colors using CMYK.

RGBA: Red, Green, Blue, and Alpha.

Rhythm: The repetition of a character's motion.

RIAA: Recording Industry Association of America.

Rich Media: Typically, a Website or banner ad that uses technology more advanced than standard GIF animation. Rich-media banners include: Flash, Shockwave, streaming video, Real Audio/Video, pull-down menus, search boxes, applets that allow for interactivity, and other types of special effects.

Right-Handed Coordinate System: The values on the X-axis (horizontal) become larger to the right of the origin; the values on the Y-axis (vertical) increase as they move above the origin; the values on the Z-axis (depth) become larger as they near.

Ring Array: A ring of four cubes rotating around a central cube.

Ripping: The process used to convert a CD file to a WAV file. The resulting WAV file is then encoded into an MP3 file.

Ripple Filter: A filter that creates fluid ripples in an image, simulating water waves.

RLE: See Run Length Coding.

Road Map: The writer's outline.

Roll: A camera rotation around its Z-axis (depth).

Rollover: A term used to describe a Website button or graphic that changes when the pointer is above it.

Root: The most dominate object in a hierarchy.

Rotation Range: Range that restricts the rotation of the joint between a minimum and maximum values.

Rotation: The movement of an element or group of elements around a specific center and axis; complete circle movement of a camera to create a spinning effect; a partial rotation is called a Tilt.

Rotoscope: A device patented by Max Fleischer in 1917, which projects live-action film, one frame at a time, onto a small screen from the rear. Drawing paper is placed over the screen allowing the animators to trace the live action images as a guide in capturing complicated movements.

Rotoscoping: A form of delaying motion capture. The Frame-by-frame projection of a live-action scene in order to trace the movements of objects. It's a method of capturing live action one frame at a time.

Rough Drawing: A term that refers to the line quality of a drawing. The animators usually draw the "roughs" and leave the finished drawings" to their inbetweeners, or people who simply "clean-up" their roughs. Many animators enjoyed doing their own finished drawings.

Roughs: The animators' original drawings, which are usually broad and sketchy to be refined by the cleanup artist.

Round Robin of Villains: A term used to describe a series in which there are several rotating villains.

Rounding: A form of beveling that literally rounds the straight edges or points of an object

Royalty: Free photos or images sold for a single standard fee that may be used repeatedly by the purchaser.

RTP (Real-time Transfer Protocol): A transport protocol created to deliver live media to one or more viewers simultaneously; used as the transfer protocol for RTSP streaming.

RTSP (Real-time Streaming Protocol): A popular standard used to transmit true streaming media to one or more viewers simultaneously. It provides for viewers randomly accessing the stream, and uses RTP.

Run-Length Encoding (RLE): Created specifically for compression and decompression of animation clips; best used as a lossless codec of sequences of drawn or rendered still images. Also known as Animation.

Running Gag: A gag that repeats through a scene, episode or series.

Runtime Code: Program code that allows playback or delivery of a program without requiring the parent application.

S

Safe Areas: The regions of the screen that will not appear cropped when shown on different television monitors.

Sample: The measurement of a signal level at a specific time.

Sample Rate: The number of samples per second used for audio. A higher sample rates yield higher quality audio that is larger than that of lower sample rates; common multimedia sample rates include 11.025 kHz, 22.050 kHz, and 44.100 kHz.

Sample Size: The accuracy with which a sound sample is recorded—generally 8 or 16 bits; the latter is more accurate and provides more dynamic range, but uses more storage space.

Sample Script: A written script used to display writing talents.

Samples Per Inch: See SPI.

Sampling: The process of reading sound waves at regular intervals, and storing the information in a digitized file. When converting video or audio waves to digital format, digitizing software chooses points along the wave and records or "snapshots" them, which can then be replayed similar to the way that motion pictures are recreated from the individual frames.

Sampling Precision: The amount of sample information stored. Typical rates are 8-bit (gives up to 256 different levels) and 16-bit (gives up to 65,536 different levels).

Saturation: The color intensity of an image; the higher the saturation, the brighter the image. An image with no saturation is also referred to as a grayscale image.

Scalable Vector Graphics (SVG): A new language standard used to describe 2D graphics in XML.

Scaling: A change in the size and/or proportion of an element or group of elements.

Scan: To create a digital file of an analog item. For example, to scan a picture.

Scan Conversion: A change of video signals from one form (RGB) to another (NTSC, PAL).

Scan Line: The parallel lines on a video screen, from upper left to lower right, along which the scanner travels to pickup and lay down video information.

Scan Line Order: A way to arrange image data so that all pixels for one scan line are stored or transmitted before the pixels for the next scan line.

Scan Rate: A rate that expresses the frequency of a signal coming out of a computer.

Scanner: A computer device that "reads" text or graphics and converts them into digitized documents/files. Most scanners light an image and measure the light reflected through it. It then converts the reflections into distinct voltages, which are transformed into patterns of dots. The resolution or clarity of the image is measured in dots per inch.

scanner

Scanning: The process of transferring film footage into a computer, usually by moving horizontally across the image with a beam of electrons.

Scene: A single measurement of a film that depicts a single situation or incident. A scene changes any time the story moves to a new location or a new time.

Scintillation: The "sparkling" of textures or small objects, usually undesirable and caused by aliasing.

Scissors Clip: A process that tests pixel coordinates against clip rectangles and rejects them if outside.

Scratch Disk: Hard-drive storage space designated as work space for processing operations, and for temporarily storing part of an image, as well as a backup version, when there is insufficient RAM. Also known as Virtual Memory.

Screen Angles: Angles used in film production for positioning halftone screens to minimize undesirable dot patterns.

Screen Directions: Directions written in capital letters. These are shots listed in the script to visually guide the animator. For example, CU (a close up) or LS (a long shot).

Screen Font: A part of the font suitcase (of Adobe Type 1 fonts), it describes the shape of each character to the operating system so that the font can be seen on screen.

Screen Frequency: The resolution (density of dots) on a halftone screen, measured in lines per inch. Also known as Screen Ruling.

Screen Narration: The information spoken to the audience by a character, or written visually on the screen.

Screen Resolution: A term that refers to the number of pixels displayed on a computer monitor; the higher the number, the more lines per inch are created on the screen.

Screen Saver: A program that replaces the image displayed on a monitor with a shifting/moving pattern that prevents the monitor from being etched by a still image.

Screening: The process of converting an image to patterns of black or white dots that can be commercially printed. Color is split into primaries then individually screened—those screens are then printed and the original color image reappears.

Screenplay: A written document that tells a story by using descriptions, dialog, and some production notes.

Script: The text of a film, giving dialog, action, staging, camera moves, etc.

Scroll: To view page parts below or above what is seen on the screen.

SCSI (Small Computer Interface): Pronounced "skuzzy," it is a more expensive interface than IDE, and not as common on Windows computers, but a standard for Macintosh computers.

Sealant: Any of a number of glues, lacquers, or adhesives, which have been used to prevent paint from cracking, chipping or peeling. Sealant can often harm other aspects of the cel, such as color or texture.

Search Engine: A program or system that searches documents on the Web for specified keywords, returning a list results containing keyword locations.

SECAM: A video standard similar to PAL, which is used in a limited number of countries.

Second Person VR: The use of a computational medium to portray a representation that is not necessarily realistic, but identifiable (puppet, avatar, vactor). For example, in the Mandala system, a video camera allows you to see yourself as another object that is controlled by your own body movement.

Secondary Action Area: A location in the scene into which some of the action eventually spills.

Secondary Motion: The motion that carries the action forward.

Secondary Scatter: Light that is reflected from a non-emitting object that illuminates other objects. It's the type of inter-object illumination that is computed by radiosity.

Segue: To switch to a new scene.

Selection: An isolated area of an image to be modified while the rest of the image is protected. Selection is also the moving marquee that denotes the boundary of a selection can be moved independently of its pixel content.

Self-Contained: A movie is self-contained when it does not contain any references to data in external files. If it is not flattened, it may contain multiple references to the same data inside the movie file, and it can contain non-referenced data.

Semi-Conductor: A limited conductivity material.

Sensor Lagtime: Delays in the feedback or representation of actions caused by computation in the tracker or sensor.

Sensors: The mechanisms or functions that act to change objects in response to multiple devices connected to lights, objects, or viewpoints in the real world.

Sensory Substitution: The conversion of sensory information from one sense to another. For example, the use of auditory echoes and cues to "see" the shape of one's surroundings.

Separation, Lifting, or Glassing: A term that refers to the separation of paint from the back of the cel, with or without cracking; separated sections appear discolored.

Sequence: A succession of camera shots connected because they develop the same aspect or moment of the action. Sequence also describes a group of related scenes combined in a film to tell a particular story, and which are usually set in the same location or time.

Sequencer: A digital device used to record, edit, or play MIDI data sequentially.

Sequences of Still Images: Sequences based on the techniques of traditional cel animation.

Serial Number: In MusicMatch Jukebox, the CD identifier used by Websites. This information is automatically pulled from a CD when the MP3 files are created; the serial number can frequently be found on the CD jacket or insert.

Serial Ports: Ports used for two-way communication that transfer data one bit at a time. Many devices, including modems, scanners, and laser printers, connect to serial ports.

Sericel: A limited-edition cel produced by serigraphing, it's a screen-printing process. To produce a sericel, a hand-cut master is prepared for each color from original studio art. The serigrapher applies each color separately, one screen at a time in perfect registration. Edition sizes for these works are generally 2,500 to 9,500. Also known as Serigraph or Seriocel.

Serigraph: Serigraphy, the printing term for the silk-screen process, is a fine-art process in which limited editions are created by meticulously screening the colors of an image onto the back of an acetate cel or the surface of fine-art paper or canvas—one color at a time. The image is separated into its individual colors then each is transferred onto a stretched screen of silk that acts as a stencil. Also known as Sericel or Siriocel.

Server API: A published interface allowing software developers to write programs that become part of the Web server. See also API.

Set: A term derived from "setting"; the prepared stages on which the action for 3D animation takes place.

Setting a Face: The process of turning 2D outlines into planes to be rendered.

Set-up Engine: An engine that allows drivers to pass polygons to the rendering engine in the form of raw vertex information, subpixel polygon addresses. A set-up engine moves processing from the host CPU to the graphics chip, reducing bus bandwidth requirements by 30% for small, randomly placed triangles, and by proportionately more for larger polygons.

Shade: To add black to a color.

Shaders: The part of a rendering program that assigns surface properties to objects by calculating the effects of illumination on the surface. Shaders are also small programs that algorithmically generate textures based on mathematical formulas.

Shading: A term used in computer graphics. It's always related to determining pixel color values, rather than the geometry of which pixels are to be drawn.

Shadow: The darkest area of an image.

Shadow Map: A map that consists of soft, fuzzy, foggy shadows to provide a realistic appearance of just one light source.

Shadow Mask: A method of construction for a display or cathode ray tube (CRT).

Shadow Ray: A shot from a specific point to the center of each light source in the scene.

Shape Interpolation: The shape of an object may change over time by interpolating between key shapes, which usually have the same topology. For example, they must contain the same number of control points in the same order.

Shared Worlds: Virtual environments shared by multiple participants at the same location or across long-distance networks.

Shareware: A program allowing one to try software before purchase . If the software is adopted then the user is expected to pay the author in the form of a registration fee.

Sharpening: A filter that increases contrast between pixels, resulting in a sharper-looking image.

Shell: The surface of an object.

Shininess: A surface attribute related to size and sharpness of the specular component.

Shockwave: A Macromedia Director program designed to view Web pages with multimedia objects, such as audio, animation, and video, and processes user actions such as mouse clicks. It's now freely available as a plug-in for Netscape Navigator and Internet Explorer Web browsers.

Shopping Cart: A listing of items selected by a consumer from an e-commerce site prior to final purchase.

Short: A term that refers to cartoons made in Hollywood studios during the 1930s, 1940s, and 1950s, which were six or seven minutes long.

Shot: An unbroken film segment; the basic component of a scene.

Show Reel: An animator's sample reel of film.

Shutter Glasses: LCD screens or physically rotating shutters used to see stereoscopically when linked to the frame rate of a monitor.

Shutter Priority: A mode in which a desired shutter speed is manually selected and locked in; the camera then chooses an appropriate lens opening (f-stop) for proper exposure. Used primarily to prevent motion-blur in fast-moving subjects/objects.

Siblings: Objects placed in the same branch of the hierarchy.

Sidekick: A character that interacts only with the hero or villain.

SIGGRAPH (Special Interest Group Graphics of the Association for Computing Machinery): Currently, the largest organization devoted to computer graphics and animation. The organization holds yearly conferences in the Summer.

Signal: The song, music or other sound recorded on a track.

Signal-to-Noise Ratio: A term used to describe, in a video signal, the ration of undesired noise to desired picture information, expressed in decibels (DB).

Signature Line: A line of dialog that identifies with only one character.

Silhouette Animation: A type of cutout animation in which only the shapes of the figures are shown against a background.

Silicon: A nonmetallic element used in the semiconductor industry as a substrate for multiple layers of materials on which electrical circuits are created.

Silicon Chip: A chip composed of millions of microscopic electronic switches.

SIMNET: (SIMulator NETworking): The advanced technology development of large-scale, fully interactive, widely distributed simulations created by ARPA with significant Army participation, and executed by scientists and engineers from BBN and Perceptronics.

Simple Motion: Motion that consists of one object, or portion, moving in one direction.

Simple Profile: Streams of MPEG that use only I- and P-frames, using less buffer memory for decoding.

Simulation: The use of images and sound to represent a situation or an event with a degree of realism.

Simulator Networking: See SIMNET.

Simulator Sickness: The disturbances produced by simulators, ranging in degree from a feeling of unpleasantness, disorientation and headaches to nausea and vomiting. Many factors may be involved, including sensory distortions such as abnormal movement of arms and heads because of the weight of equipment. Simulator Sickness may also be long delays or lags in feedback, and missing visual cues from convergence and accommodation; It rarely occurs with displays less than 60 degrees visual angle.

Sizes: 12-field cel or drawing of 10"x12"; 16-field cel or drawing of 12"x16"; Pan (cinemascope) cel or drawing up to 12"x30".

Skeleton: The controlling structure used to pose a character.

Skin Surfaces: The surface covering the skeleton.

Skins: A way for users to alter the screen appearance of a program.

Slider: A method of entering numeric values used in GUIs (graphic user interfaces). By moving sliders back and forth, numeric values can be adjusted.

Slip-cuing: Method of cueing records which involves moving the record forwards and backwards until the precise starting point of a selection is found. Allows for the instantaneous start of a selection.

Slit-Scan: A form of controlled streak photography whereby dramatic abstract effects can be achieved by shooting suitable artwork through a slit while at least two of the key physical elements (camera, slit, artwork) are in motion during the course of a long exposure.

Slope: The rate of change in a curve over time.

Slot Mask: A method of guiding electron beams in a picture.

Slow In/Slow Out: A term that refers to planning and trucking moves that begin slowly, gradually attain full speed then slow to a stop—to avoid a sense of jerkiness in movement.

Slow Synch: A flash mode in which the image is given some exposure before or after the flash is fired, so as to bring out details in the background that would normally be underexposed or not recorded at all.

Slugline: The line that introduces each scene; It always written in capital letters and includes whether the scene is exterior or interior, its location, and the time of day. For example, INT. SEWER PIPES: MIDNIGHT or EXT. CENTRAL PARK: LATE AFTERNOON.

Small Computer Interface: See SCSI.

SmartMedia: A postage stamp-sized memory card used by some digicam manufacturers as an alternative to Compact Flash cards; presently capable of storing up to 64MB of digital image information. Also known as SSDFC or Solid State Floppy Disk Card.

SMIL (Synchronized Multimedia Integration Language): A markup language developed by the World Wide Web Consortium (W3C) enabling Web developers to divide multimedia content into separate files and streams (audio, video, text, and images), send them to a user's computer individually, and then have them displayed together as if they were a single multimedia stream. The ability to separate the static text and images makes the multimedia content much smaller, taking less time to travel the Internet.

Smooth Surface Shading: Assigns a continuous shading value that blends throughout the visible polygons on the surface.

Smoothing: A filter that averages pixels with their neighbor, reducing contrast and simulating an out-of-focus image.

SND: A sound file format for the Macintosh System 7 or later.

Solorization: The photographic effect of reducing the number of colors in an image.

Sound Card: A circuit board added to the motherboard of a microcomputer, it generates audio signals and provides output to headphones or external speakers.

Sound: The audio portion of a film, which consists of three components: music, sound effects and video (either dialog or narration).

Sound Effects: The sounds heard in a cartoon.

Space Subdivision Modeling: A modeling technique in which the scene is broken into small regions of space; it is a list of the objects present is kept for each region. For example, BSP trees and octrees.

Space-Oriented Procedural Techniques: Techniques based on the effect of the surrounding environment.

Spam (or Spamming): The Internet version of junk mail. Spamming also means to send the same message to a large number of users, usually as advertising.

Span: In raster graphics architecture, a primitive is formed by scan conversion wherein each scan line intersects the primitive at two ends, P left and P right.

Spatial Aliasing: When spatial resolution of an image is too low, details are often lost.

Spatial Compression: A method of removing redundant data within an image. For example, a field of blue in a picture would be stored as one large blue area rather than many individual blue pixels.

Spatial Navigation: A type of navigation that is accurate self-localization and orientation in virtual spaces but is not as easy as real world navigation.

Spatial Representation System: The cortical and other neural structures and functions that maintain spatial orientation and recognition.

Spatial Resolution: The number of lines or dots used to define an image.

Spatial Superposition: In augmented reality display, the accurate spatial registration of real and virtual images remains difficult.

Spatial Textures: Textures that exist in 3D space and affect the spatial integrity of the smooth surface of an object.

Speaker: An out jack that allows one to plug the sound card into a set of unamplified speakers and run them from the sound card's internal amplifier.

Spec Script: A script written in hopes of selling on speculation.

Spectrum: The range of colors on a given palette.

Specular: The highlight or reflection on a 3D surface.

Specular Reflection: Reflection that appears very shiny because they reflect light the way a mirror does.

Specular Surface Shading: Shading that creates surfaces with highlights found in reflective surfaces.

Sphere Filter: A special-effect filter that simulates wrapping the current image around a 3D sphere.

Spheres: Objects modeled as symmetric, closed, 3D objects.

Spherical Environment Mapping: Mapping that is based on a flat image that is first projected on the inside of a sphere that represents the environment.

Spherical Projection: Projection that applies a rectangular map by wrapping it around a surface until the opposite sides meet, then pinching it at the top and bottom, and stretching it until the four sides of the map are pressed together.

Spherical/Azimuthal Coordinate System: A system that provides a simple way of placing objects in a 3D world in terms of their distance to the object, their angle around the point of interest, and their altitude angle above the point of interest.

SPI (Samples Per Inch): Scanners may be described as having a certain DPI resolution, however, the scanner captures a certain number of samples per inch of a scanned image.

Spider/Robot: A software program used by search engines that visit every site on the Web, following all of the links and cataloguing all the text of each page.

Spirals: 2D, open contours. These require a starting and ending radius, a starting and ending angle, a number of control points, and a height.

Splice: To join two pieces of film, either photographically or magnetically.

Spline: A type of model created by a sequence of straight or curved lines connected to each other at Control Vertices (CV), which controls the shape of the curve.

Spline Patch: A curved surface which takes its shape from the placement of a set of control points.

Split Fields: A term that refers to the way a video image was captured. A split field occurs when one image equals two fields, which are stored as two separate pictures, one for each field.

Spoof: To poke fun of something or someone in a good-natured manner.

Spot Color: A custom-mixed ink color used in printing. A separate plate is used to print each spot color; pantone is a commonly used spot color matching system. Each spot channel holds data for an individual custom color. See also Process Color.

Spotlight: A light that casts cone-shaped light in one specific direction.

Spotlight Source: A light source that does not shine in all directions, but rather in a cone shape. It is a convenient hack for modeling lamps with shades or reflectors, without actually having to compute the effect of the shade or reflector during rendering.

Springboard: A three- to six- sentence idea, which includes the story plot and what the character will accomplish, and combines the moral and central idea. It has a beginning, middle and end, and should capture the tone of the cartoon series.

Sprite: A 2D image that can move over a background without disruption.

Sprite Track: A QuickTime track made of small graphic elements that have associated position and time information. For example, a bouncing ball.

Squash and Stretch: The judicial squashing or stretching of a character in motion, exaggerating the normal tendency of an object in motion to undergo a degree of distortion, lengthening as it travels and compressing as it stops.

Stabilization: The ability to take movement out of a series of images by locking into an object within the image.

Staging: The planning of how the action will take place.

Stand: The entire photographing unit, including the compound, camera, and crane.

Standard General Markup Language: See SGML.

Starsight: A subscription-based electronic program guide that allows users to sort the guide by order of preference and delete stations never watched.

Static Mask: A media cleaner feature that composites defined areas of an image across frames to improve temporal compression.

Status Bar: An information bar common in graphical user interfaces (GUI).

Stencil Buffer: A buffer that holds special information for each pixel as to whether or not to draw it.

Stereopsis: Binocular vision of images with horizontal disparities; the importance of stereopsis for immersion is not established.

Stereoscopic: An image or viewing system that appears to produce a 3D scene, which gives the illusion of depth.

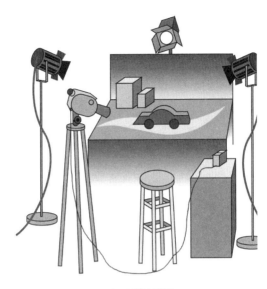

stopmotion setup

Stop Bit: A control bit that signifies the end of an asynchronous character in data transmission; always the binary digit 0.

Stop Motion: The animation of 3D objects by moving them slightly before each exposure; the method used to animate by photographing the scene one frame at a time, and changing the position of the moving characters or objects in small increments. Also known as Stop Action.

Story Editor: A person who develops and oversees the cartoon series.

Story Sketch: See Storyboard.

Storyboard: A sequence of graphic representations, often with dialog or captions, displaying important scenes. A visual interpretation of the screenplay, it contains many images and production notes. A Storyboard is a series of small consecutive drawings with accompanying caption-like descriptions of the action and sound, which are arranged in comic-strip fashion and used to plan a film.

Storyboard Drawing: A drawing(s) used to visually describe the plot of a film, typically depicting the overall theme or scenario of a brief moment in the film. When viewed together, the directors and lead animators can edit the story before animation begins. Storyboard drawings are usually smaller than standard 12-field animation drawings, depending on the studio, year, and production.

Streak Photography: The results obtain from fast moving lights, such as a car head light, and a slow shutter speed photograph. The camera employs exposure times long enough to cause the lights to smear.

Streaming: The process of playing sounds and video in real time while downloading—useful for reproduction and distribution of radio broadcasts.

Street: In film, one street equals one scene, or a series of very short scenes.

Stretch (Speed up/Slow down): In animation, stretch refers to the elongation of a character or object to give the illusion that it is accelerating.

Striate Cortex: Visual cortex. See Occipital, Parietal.

Stripe: To record time code, usually SMPTE, on a channel of the tape prior to editing.

Strobing: The jerky movement of objects in a scene due to lack of sufficient motion blur.

Structure-Oriented Procedural Techniques: Techniques based on the internal conditions.

Studio Background: A non-production background prepared by the studio for publicity or presentation purposes.

stylus and tablet

Stylus: An input device in the form of a pen-shaped instrument used to enter, draw lines, or point to choices on a computer screen.

Subassembly: An individually replaceable component integrated with other components to form a system.

Subdirectory: A data structure in the Microsoft DOS and Windows filing systems that represents a division of the root directory.

Subject of a Screenplay: This term is defined by what the story is about, who the characters are, and what happens to them throughout the sequence of events.

Submenu: A lower-level menu or series of choices at which the user arrives after selecting a main menu choice that branches to the submenu.

Subnetwork: A small network linked with other networks by a router or bridge.

Subpixel: An input pixel to an operation that uses multiple smaller pixels at higher a resolution to compute each resulting pixel at the final resolution. For example, an anti-aliasing filtering operation.

Subpixel Positioning: A technique used to break up pixels into smaller subpixels in memory so that a line can be drawn to the nearest subpixel.

Subsample: When capturing data, it refers to discarding portions of a signal for the purpose of reducing the amount of data to be compressed.

Subtractive Color: Assuming a white background, the mixture of various intensities of the colors cyan, magenta, and yellow to produce all visible colors.

Subtractive Color Mixing: A color model that mixes in a way that simulates how pigments (paint) work when different colored pigments are mixed together.

Supercomputers: Computers that are larger and more expensive than mainframes, that have an emphasis on speed and performance.

Super-Microcomputers (workstations): Microcomputers built around a powerful CPU customized to excel in the performance of a specific task.

Super-VGA (SVGA): A video monitor/card supporting 640x480 resolution (or greater) with 256 colors or more.

SureStream: RealSystem G2 scalability feature, which allows multiple versions of a file to be encoded and delivered to users based on their connection.

Surface: A term defined by the position of its bounding lines.

Surface Illumination: Illumination that controls the degree by which the maps blend with the surface by splitting it in terms of ambient, diffuse and specula areas or the surface illumination.

Surface Libraries: A term that refers to when shader includes only the characteristics of the surface material.

Surface Mapping: Often when objects are to be rendered in order to achieve a more realistic look, a surface map is applied to an object. It's a picture which is wrapped around an object in one or more fashions.

Surface Mount: A term related to PC-board assembly, a technique for high-density manufacturing using a variety of semiconductor packages.

Surface Normals: Vectors or straight lines with a specific direction.

Surface of Revolution: Surfaces created with a lathe.

Surface Properties: The collective name for all object-specific parameters used to compute the apparent color of an object point, such as the diffuse color and specular color. The term is common but not standard. Also known as Visual Properties or Material Properties.

Surface Transparency: Represented by simulating the behavior of light on transparent materials.

Surge Protector: A device used to monitor the level of electrical current between a power source and a computer or other electronic component.

Surrogate Travel: A VR system in which point-of-view travel is simulated, allowing the user to control the path taken through the environment.

Sustained Transfer Rate: The number of bytes per second (bps) a CD-ROM drive, or other storage medium, can deliver as it reads data objects larger than its internal buffer.

SVG (Scalable Vector Graphics): A new language standard used to describe 2D graphics in XML.

SVG: See Scalable Vector Graphics.

SVGA: See Super-VGA.

Sweeting: In video or film post-production, this terms refers to the development of an audio track with mixed elements, such as music, sound effects, and applause.

Switch: A device that opens or closes circuitry.

Sword of Damocles: The nickname for the first helmet-mounted display at the University of Utah (Sutherland).

Sync Stripper: A video signal contains video information, which is the picture to be displayed, and timing (sync) information that tells the receiver where to put this video information on the display. A sync stripper selects the sync information from the video signal and tosses the rest.

Synching: In this process, dialog is often recorded separately from the picture, most commonly on tape or DAT.

Synchronization: The coordination of sound and picture, matched precisely in the finished film. Also known as Sync.

Synchronized Multimedia Integration Language: See SMIL.

Synthesized: Sounds created by computer circuitry.

Synthesizer: An electronic device with associated software used to create sound effects.

Synthetic Environments: VR displays used for simulation.

T

T-1 Carrier: 1,544 MBps; a dedicated phone connection (DS1 line) supporting the fastest speed commonly used to connect networks to the Internet.

T-1, T-3 Line: High-speed digital lines that provide data communication speeds of 1,544 megabits (T-1) and 45 megabits (T-3) per second. A T-1 line consists of 24 individual channels, each of which supports 64 Kbps and each 64 Kbps channel can be configured to carry voice or data traffic.

T-3 Carrier: A dedicated phone connection (DS3 line), used mainly by ISPs, to the Internet backbone, able to carry 45 MBps, enough for full-screen, full-motion video.

Tablet: A devices used along with a stylus to input information into a computer. The tablet simulates a drawing pad and the stylus a pen. This device is commonly used by artist and designers to input drawings.

Tactile Displays: Devices such as force feedback gloves, buzzers and exoskeletons that provide tactile, kinaesthetic and joint sensations. See also Tactile Stimulation.

Tag: The description given to a character when first introduced. The tag is not capitalized, but the character's name is (only the first time s/he appears on the page).

Tagged Image File Format: See TIFF.

Tagging: The process of saving additional information in an MP3 file, such as e-mail, artist bio, lyrics, and URL. The two common types of tagging are: MusicMatch and ID3.

Take: A reaction by a character.

Talking Heads: A term that refers to when cartoon characters sit or stand while chatting—with no movement other than facial expressions.

Tangent: The slope of a curve at a specific point.

Targa: A raster graphics file format developed by Truevision, Inc. It uses .TGA file extension, and handles 16-, 24-, and 32-bit color. It's also the trade name of a line of video graphics boards used in high-resolution imaging.

Target Age: The age a character tries to reach in a script.

TCP (Transfer Control Protocol): A common network transfer protocol used widely on the Internet.

TD: See Technical Director.

Teaser: A scene, or series of short scenes, that introduce the cartoon episode in an exciting way to grab the audience's attention.

Technical Director (TD): The individual who operates the control room switcher and is in charge of various technical aspects of a production.

Technoetics: Technology that works directly with the human consciousness.

Telecine: A device that transfers film footage to video.

Teleconference: A telephone meeting wherein callers can see and hear each other.

Tele-Existence: Remote VR.

Tele-Immersion: A technology to be implemented with Internet2 that will enable users in different geographic locations to interact in a simulated environment.

Telemanipulation: The robotic control of distant objects.

Telematics: The art of communication, not only including Internet, but also phone, fax, and satellite links.

Teleoperation: See Telemanipulation.

Telephoto 135 mm Lens: A close-framing lens.

Teleplay: A script written exclusively for television.

Telepresence: Work that entails operation at a distance.

Telerobotic: The robotic control of distant objects. See also Telemanipulation and Teleoperation.

Temp Mix: A temporary soundtrack with simple effects and music used to show a commercial, movie trailer, film, or video program before it is entirely ready.

Tempo: Another term for pace.

Temporal Aliasing: Aliasing in time by animation frame, instead of spatially by pixel; the visual effect of temporal aliasing has been called "strobing." It involves moving objects appear to jump through a sequence of frozen steps, rather than in smooth paths.

Temporal Compression: Video compression that compares frames, transmitting only the differences between them. Also known as Interframe Compression.

Terrain: Geographical information and models either randomly generated or based on actual data; dynamic terrain is an important goal for current SIMNET applications.

Tessellation: The act of tiling a surface with individual patches.

Tessellation Level: The relative fineness or granularity of the patches used to model a surface. A model with smaller, and therefore more, patches is said to have a higher tessellation level.

Tetrahedron: A four-sided rectangular polyhedral.

Texel: One pixel of a texture map image; in diffuse color texture mapping, the texture value is a color—the texture color values are therefore often supplied as an image.

Text Files: Files that contain no special codes or commands, such as bold, italics, or graphics—only text. Unlike binary files, text files can be read with no special software.

Text Track: A track made up of text, style, positioning, and time information. QuickTime text tracks are often used for subtitles.

Text-to-Speech: Voice synthesizers that "read" computer text. First used to read screens for blind computer users, text-to-speech is becoming increasingly popular for children's games.

Texture Anti-Aliasing: An interpolation technique used to remove texture distortion, stair-casing, or jagged edges, at the edges of an object.

Texture Filtering: The process of removing the undesirable distortion of a raster image. Also referred to as aliasing artifacts, such as sparkles and blockiness, through interpolation of stored texture images.

Texture Map: The external function that supplies the texture value in texture mapping. In diffuse color texture mapping, the texture map is a set of color values in two dimensions.

Texture Mapping: The process of applying a 2D image to a 3D object defined within the computer, similar to wrapping wallpaper around an object.

object   texture   texture map

Texture Memory: Section of the memory used to store the texture maps.

Texture Swimming: Unnatural motion of static textures on the surfaces of objects as they are rotated—caused by quick and dirty texture interpolation in screen coordinates. It's correctable by subdividing polygons sufficiently, or by perspective correction.

TFT (Thin Film Transistor): A type of digicam monitor display that allows a wider, brighter viewing angle than a standard LCD monitor.

TGA: See Targa.

Thaumatrope: An early animation device that consisted of a disc with one image painted on each side. When the disc was spun on a loop of string, the images seemed to appear together.

Thickness: A term defined by the distance between the front face and the back face of a surface.

Thin Film Transistor: See TFT.

Thought Process: A process that provides clues and insight about characters' fate and possible development of the story.

Thrash: When you run out of hardware memory, an advanced operating system will free up memory space by moving the contents of some of your memory to disk. When the information is needed again, it is read from disk back into memory. When a computer is thrashing, memory is being swapped back and forth at such a rate that the hard drive is constantly spinning, preventing the computer from performing additional tasks at that time.

Thread: A series of messages (related to the same topic) in a discussion or news group.

Thumbnail: A low-resolution version of an image, used to give the user an idea of what the full-resolution image will look like.

Ticking Clock: A story device that creates tension as well as a need for immediate character action. It forces a character to perform a certain action by a specific time, or a grave consequence will occur.

TIFF (Tagged Image File Format): A common file format used to store both raster and vector graphics information.

Tiling: A process that creates patterns by repeating a tile of a single rectangular image map.

Tilt: A rotation of the camera on its horizontal axis.

Timebase Corrector: Certain video sources have incorrect sync signals, the most common of which is the VCR. It fixes a video signal that has bad sync timing.

Time-Based Art: Art that cannot be grasped synchronically. For example, video.

Timecode: A means of marking single frames of video or film. It's a number in the form of HH:MM:SS:FF (hours, minutes, seconds, and frames) that designates a single frame in a video or film sequence.

Timeline: A graphical representation of a sequence of frames.

Timing: The lab's process of selecting printing lights to for the proper rendition of exposure and color when making a print. The term is a little confusing, as it has nothing at all to do with "time" as in "running time" or such.

Tint: To add white to a color.

Title Bar: The top bar across any window in a graphical user interface (GUI).

Title Cards: A background painting that acts as part of the credits for an animated film. The text is often on a cel overlay. Title cards can be divided into several categories: Series Title, Main, Cast and Crew Credits.

Title Safe Area: The central region of the screen where text is most readable. See also Action Safe, Safe Areas, and Overscan.

Toggle: A small triangle-shaped button, which rotates to reveal more information in Media Cleaner's interface. Similar to "disclosure triangles" in the Finder, which allows one to view the contents of a folder without first opening it. Clicking once reveals more information, while clicking again hides the extra information.

Tolerance: The range of pixels a tool operates within. For example, the range of shades or colors the Magic Wand tool selects, or the Paint Bucket tool fills.

Tone: Hue with additional black and white.

Toner: The material deposited onto the page forming the image in a photocopier or laser printer.

Topper: A gag or line of dialog that "out-does," or "tops" the previous gag.

Torus: A 3D closed shape resembling a donut.

Tow-Away Street: The story's catalyst; the scene in Act One in which the driver is towed or pulled into the story.

Trace Contour: A filter used to find and trace edges while making all solid colors the same.

Track: Entire songs (MP3 or WAV files, or original cuts for cassettes, vinyl, or CDs). The term track is old industry jargon from radio, DJs, and the music business. When speaking of mixing and audio production, however, the term refers to a single signal or set of signals in an unmixed recording, such as the lyrics track, the drum track, or the bass track—these tracks are then mixed into the completed song.

Tracker: A device that emits numeric coordinates for the changing position in space.

Tracking: The automatic following of a point(s) in a shot.

Traffic Node: A group of information pages on a Website.

Transcode: A term generally used to mean "recompression," but can also mean "Lossless Format Conversion."

Transfer Control Protocol: See TCP.

Transformation Matrix: Aides programs in the calculation of geometric transformations.

Transition: In computer animation, transitions are ways of moving from one picture to another. Examples of transitions are fading, wiping, morphing, and blending.

Transition Morphing: The process of cross-fading from one image to another while warping the two images to appear as if they are transforming into one another.

Translation: The movement of an object(s) in a linear way to a new location in the 3D space.

Translucent: Partially transparent quality of materials that modify the light passing through in a more complicated way than simple color filtering.

Transparency: A term that refers to how invisible and unobtrusive a VR system can be.

Transparency Map: A monochromatic surface with the purpose of making all or some of the surface transparent.

Transparent: Allows light to pass through.

Transterritorial: Beyond physical space. For example, Cyberspace.

Traveling Mattes: A matte is a mask that blocks off a predetermined part of a photographic image. Traveling mattes are masks that move and change from frame to frame. Blue screen is used to reduce the actor or miniature to a sequence of moving silhouette masks which are then used to "cutout windows" into suitable background plates.

Traveling Peg Bars: See Panning Peg Bars.

Traveling Shot: A term that refers to the use of a dolly following along side the subject.

Treatment: The third phase in the animation writing process.

Triangle Strip Primitive: A graphic primitive that contains a set of successively abutting triangles. A triangle strip primitive is more efficient than the equivalent separate triangle primitives. Also known as Tstrip.

Tri-Linear MIP Mapping: A method of reducing aliasing artifacts within texture maps by applying a bilinear filter to four texels from the two nearest MIP maps, and then interpolating between the two.

Trimmed: A cel that has had some portion(s) removed.

Trimmed Surface: Surfaces created with trimming.

Trojan Horse Virus: A virus that pretends to be something it is not. Typically, Trojan Horses Viruses take the form of a game that deletes files while the user plays.

Trompe l'Oeil: Perspective paintings that deceive viewers into believing they are real. For example, a painting of the sky and clouds on the inside of a dome.

Truck: A camera move in which the camera seems to move closer (Truck In) or away from (Truck out) the subject.

True Color: Color depth of 24 bits (16.7 million colors).

True Streaming: A term that refers to technologies that match the bandwidth of the media signal to the viewer's connection, so that the media is always seen in real time. The word "true" is added to differentiate this type of streaming from "HTTP Streaming" (Also known as "Progressive Download"). Specialized media servers and streaming protocols, such as RTSP, are required to enable true streaming.

Try-Fails: Gag sequences in which a character repeatedly tries to achieve a goal, fails, then tries again and fails again…

Turnaround: A state of limbo that a movie enters after a studio decides to drop it. In turnaround, the producers have a chance to set the project up with another studio or with different talent.

Turnaround Time: The length of time taken from the start of a project to completion (submission to the editor).

Twain: Software developed by the Twain Working Group (scanner manufacturers and scanning software developers) in order to facilitate scanning of pictures. The TWAIN driver runs between the scanner hardware and the program (Photoshop or PhotoPaint, for example).

Tweak: To pull sharply with a twisting movement.

Tweening: Short for In-betweening—the process of generating intermediate frames between two images to give the appearance that the first image evolves smoothly into the second. Tweening is a key process in all types of animation. Sophisticated animation software enables identification of specific objects in an image and define how they should move and change during the tweening process.

Tweens: An image drawn to show a character between the extreme moments of action or gesture.

Typeface: Contains a series of fonts. For example, Arial contains the fonts Arial, Arial Bold, Arial Italic, and Arial Bold Italic.

U

UDP (User Datagram Protocol): A data transmission standard used by RTP for broadcasting data via IP networks. It is designed for real-time broadcast and lacks many of the error-correction features of TCP, which means UDP may lose data in transmission if there are problems with the network.

Umbra: The inner part of the shadow.

Underscan: When an image is displayed, it is "underscanned" if the entire image is visible on the display; common in computer displays.

Unicast: The delivery of a unique stream to each viewer. Because each viewer initiates a new stream when viewing the same source, this approach to media delivery can result in increased network congestion as multiple, identical streams are sent at the same time.

Uniform Resource Locator: See URL.

Unitize: To make a vector a unit vector, which means adjusting its length to be one without effecting the direction in which it is pointing.

Universal File Format: A format widely used for transporting 3D modeling information between programs.

Universal Serial Bus: See USB.

Universe: The "container" of all entities in VR.

Unsharp Mask: A mask that makes a soft image appear to have more detail than it really does.

Up Vector: A vector used to define the orientation of the virtual camera in a scene.

Upsampling: See Interpolation.

Upward Compatibility: Exists when files created with previous versions of software are compatible with new software upgrades.

URL (Uniform Resource Locator): An address referring to an HTML document on the Internet—a Website address.

USB (Universal Serial Bus): A computer port to which peripherals can be connected and, when used by a USB-equipped digicam, allows rapid transfer of digital camera images to the computer.

User Datagram Protocol: See UDP.

U-Turn: The scene that turns the story in a new or unexpected direction.

V

VACTORS: Virtual Actors, either autonomous or telerobotic, in a VR theater.

Variable Bit Rate (VBR): Maximizes audio quality without limiting the size of the resulting MP3 file; not all MP3 players can handle files recorded using VBR.

Variable Frame Length Movie: A movie that contains frames that are not all of equal duration. Supported by QuickTime, but not AVI.

VBR: See Variable Bit Rate.

VCR (Video Cassette Recorder): Often implies consumer-grade recorders with VHS or half-inch tape.

Vection: The illusion of self-motion caused by moving visual images.

Vector: A term that describes magnitude and direction.

Vector Graphics: Graphics based on individual lines from point A to point B. A graphic image drawn in shapes and lines, called paths. Images created in Illustrator and Freehand (graphic design software) are vector graphics, and are usually exported to bitmap images.

Vector Primitive: A graphics primitive resembling a line segment. Unlike Vector Scaling, the resulting vector is the same as the input vector, except that its magnitude (length) is multiplied by the scalar. Scaling a vector by the reciprocal of its magnitude results in a unit vector.

Vector Thickness: The width of a vector, or line segment. See also Vector Primitive.

Vectorscope: A hardware or software tool used to measure the color values of a video signal.

Velocity Scan Modulation: Commonly used in TVs to increase the apparent sharpness of a picture. At horizontal dark-to-light transitions, the beam scanning speed is momentarily increased approaching the transition, making the display relatively darker just before the transition. Upon passing into the lighter area, the beam speed is momentarily decreased, making the display relatively brighter just after the transition. The reverse occurs in passing from light to dark.

Vertex: a collection of three numbers that define its position in the coordinate system. Points are the building blocks of all 3D objects—from points one can build faces and meshes.

Vertical Interval Time Code: See VITC.

Vertical Retrace: The returning of a display screen or TV's electron gun to the upper-left corner—this step takes about one-sixtieth of a second.

Vestibulo-Occular Reflex (VOR): The motion of the eyes, which compensates for motions of the head to keep objects stationary within the field of view. When simulating motion in virtual environments, discrepancies between the perceived and actual motion of the head interfere with the VOR and lead to motion sickness.

Video: A series of framed images, lined up one after another, to simulate motion and interactivity. It can be transmitted by number of frames per second and/or the amount of time between switching frames. The difference between video and animation is that video is broken down into individual frames.

Video Animation Stand: A special unit designed to photograph animation on videotape. The recorder moves the tape in one-24ths-of-a-second increments that correspond to frames of film—its instant replay capacity makes it useful for pencil tests.

Video Back End: The part of a display controller that reads the pixel data in the bitmap and produces the live video signals. Among other components, the back end contains the color lookup tables (LUTs), the digital to analog converters (DACs), and the logic to generate the video timing signals.

Video Lunch Box: A device that allows animators to create stop-motion animation tests. The device is connected to a camera on one end, and video recording deck on the other; the device stores the single frame recordings in its memory for playback and possible output to the video recorder. Similar to the pencil tester for stop-motion animation.

Video Random Access Memory: See VRAM.

View Finder: A registration device mounted near the top of the animation stand that allows the camera operator to verify that the camera is trained on the center of the field.

Viewing Angle: A term that defines the size relation between the near and far clipping planes.

View-Point: The points from which raytracing and geometry creation.

Viewport: A virtual window to look inside the 3D world.

Vintage Cel: A term that refers to art from the 1920s to 1960s. These cels were hand-inked using a multitude of colored inks—very few vintage cels exist.

Vinyl- and Acrylic-Based Cel Paints: Although more durable and permanent than vintage gum Arabic-based paint formulas, they do not have as wide a variety of pigments as the traditional Disney paint formula. In most cases, the original Disney gum Arabic paint formula is preferable for archival restoration.

Virtual Cadaver: A current NIH project used to slice and digitize a human body.

Virtual Environments: Realistic simulations of interactive scenes.

Virtual Memory: Hard-drive storage space designated as work space for processing operations, and for temporarily storing part of an image, as well as a backup version, when there is insufficient RAM. Also known as Scratch Disk.

Virtual Patient: Telerobotic or digitized animations of humans with accurate disease models.

Virtual Private Network (VPN): A private network within a public network—virtual network privacy is achieved through encryption, and provides a less expensive option to using dedicated lines. See also PPTP.

Virtual Prototyping: The use of VR for design and evaluation of new artifacts.

Virtual Reality: A name loosely applied to systems that attempt to immerse the user in a computer-generated virtual world, which is often done with a stereoscopic display that is updated based on head position, and usually includes some sort of 3D pointing device. More advanced systems include 3D sound and some form of touch feedback.

Virtual Reality Alliance of Students and Professionals: See VRASP.

Virtual Reality Markup Language: See VRML.

Virtual Sculpting: Sculpting similar to the process of hand-molding fresh clay.

Visible Light Sources: Lights sources that can be seen by the camera.

Visual Effects: A group responsible for the overall production of all special effects projects. Traditionally called photographic effects or optical effects as it was originally done through the use of optic and trick photography. Today's visual effect is done via the use of computers but is still outputted to film.

Visual Line of Action: Action that determines the position and sequence of motions in the scene that will guide the eyes of the audience to different parts of the image.

Visual Textures: Flat simulations of 3D texture that do not affect the geometrical surface of the object.

Visualization: The use of computer graphics to make visible numeric or other quantifiable relationships.

VITC (Vertical Interval Time Code): Time code information in digital form inserted into two or three lines in the "vertical interval," thus avoiding the loss of an audio track or "crosstale."

VLUT: Visual Look-Up Table.

VO: See Voiceover.

Voiceover (VO): Used when a character's voice is heard, but the character is not seen on the screen or speaking the words.

Volume Shader: A term that defines the characteristics of materials in 3D space that affect light as it travels through them.

VOR: See Vestibulo-Occular Reflex.

Voxel: A cubic volume pixel used to quantize 3D space.

VPN: See Virtual Private Network.

VRAM (Video Random Access Memory): Actually DRAM—with additional features specifically for use as bitmap memory in display controllers. VRAM typically costs twice as much as DRAM, but allows the drawing engine full access to the bitmap independent from the video back end, which can increase hardware drawing rate.

VRASP (Virtual Reality Alliance of Students and Professionals): A group founded by Karin August and her cookies, to promote the ethical and socially exciting uses of VR.

VQF: A sound file format similar to MP3; VQF produces files that are half again as small as MP3 files with sound qualities that are at least as good. VQF files take longer to encode and a little more CPU power to play. They are not as popular as MP3 files.

VRML: Virtual Reality Markup Language.

W

Waist Shot: A shot that presents a character from the waist up.

Waldo: A remotely controlled mechanical puppet (Heinlein).

Walla: Short for "wall of sound," meaning the collective background sounds that a group of people make in a crowd.

WAN (Wide Area Network): Connects a large area of computers, usually more than one building.

Warp: A 2D digital effect to distort or contort an image using control points on the image to determine the way it's transformed.

Wash: To change a color by altering its hue and saturation.

WAV: (Pronounced "wave") sounds that are converted directly from an analog signal into digital sound, and stored as the component waveforms .

Web Analysis: The collection and interpretation of data about the parameters, traffic, and security of a Website, server, or network.

Web Browser: An application that enables users to find and view pages on the Internet.

Web Hosting: Supplying the infrastructure to create and maintaining Websites and online content, usually for a rental fee.

Web Tracking: Charting and analyzing the flow of user traffic to and from a Website or network.

Web-Casting: This technology publishes/broadcasts personalized information to subscribers, then, rather than using bookmarks and search engines to pull down information, users run a client application updated with data that is "pushed" down by a server. Also known as Push Web Technology or Channel-Casting.

Website: A collection of electronic pages formatted in HTML (Hypertext Markup Language) that contain text, graphic images, or multimedia effects such as sound files, video and/or animation files, and other programming elements such as Java and Javascript.

WebTV: Originally a general term for a category of products and technologies that enable one to surf the Web via TV. It makes a connection to the Internet via telephone service and then converts the downloaded Web pages to a format that can be displayed on the TV—these products also come with a remote control device to navigate the Web.

White Balance: A term that refers to how the color temperature of the scene is measured prior to exposure and electronically adjusted so that white objects will not take on excessive color casts of red, blue, or if shot under most fluorescent lighting, green.

Wide Angle: 24 or 28 mm lens, a generous 83-degree view, outstanding depth of field, small amount of distortion on the edges of the picture.

Wide Area Network: See WAN.

Wide Shot (WS): A shot that includes the entire body in the frame.

Winding Road: The subplot that winds through the story, reflecting its main plot line.

Windows: On some hardware platforms, one can have multiple windows and viewpoints into the same virtual world.

Wipes: A transition in which one scene appears to advance onto the screen over another.

Wire Frame: A simple non-shaded model that many computers can manipulate in real time.

Wire Frame Outlines: Displays of the outlines of unfilled polygons.

Workprint: A print of the film made from the original for editing purposes. When the director is satisfied with the editing of the workprint, the original will be cut to match, so that release prints can be struck.

Workspace: A 3D space that defines boundaries.

World Global Coordinate System: A system used to place or move objects in the world or in relation to each other.

World in the Hand: A metaphor used in visualized tracking—the tracker is held in the hand and is connected to motion of the object located at that position in the display.

World: The whole environment or universe.

Worm: An insidious, and usually illegal, computer program designed to replicate itself via a network for the purpose of causing harm and/or destruction. While a virus is designed to invade a single computer's hard drive, a worm is designed to invade a network. Used to describe optical disk drives that can only be written once, usually for archival purposes.

WS: See Wide Shot.

WYSIWYG: An acronym (pronounced "wizzywig") for what-you-see-is-what-you-get. Refers to a computer screen representation of text or graphics being the same as the subsequent hardcopy printout.

X

X-Bitmap: An uncompressed black-and-white image file format (.xbm).

Xerographic-Line Cel: A six-step xerographic process developed by Disney in the 1950s. Instead of hand-inking the drawings on the cels prior to painting them, the image is transferred by xerography.

Xerography: A special form of photocopying onto cels. Developed by the Disney studio in conjunction with the Xerox Company, it is used in place of inking to transfer the animation drawings onto cels.

XHTML (Extensible Hypertext Mark-up Language): A hybrid of XML and HTML. Web pages designed in XHTML should look the same across all platforms.

X-Pixelmap: An uncompressed color image file (.xpm).

X-Sheet: Exposure Sheet. It began as a place to record instructions for the camera operator, but have accumulated many uses over time. Often, they begin to take shape before final drawings are made for the film. When the soundtrack is recorded, it can be entered on the X-Sheet, using the rows of empty frames as a timeline. With spoken words spelled out vertically along the page, animators can tell on which frame they will need to draw the mouth shape corresponding to each sound.

Y

Y: The common reference for the height of an image; Y is the vertical axis.

Yaw: The angular displacement of a view around the vertical, Y-axis (verticle).

YUV: A color model that describes color information in terms of luminance (Y) and two chrominance channels (U, V); the YUV space is commonly used in video, and easily supports color subsampling.

YUV9: A color format with substantial subsampling often used with online video technologies, such as Sorenson Video; for every 16 luminance "Y" samples in a 4x4 pixel block, there is only one "U" and one "V" sample. This dramatic color subsampling produces smaller files, with correspondingly lower color fidelity; often results in noticeable color artifacts around the edges of brightly colored objects.

YUV12: Intel's notation for MPEG-1 4: 2: 0 YCbCr stored in memory in a planar format. The picture is divided into blocks, with each block comprising 2 x 2 samples. For each block, four 8-bit values of Y, one 8-bit value of Cb, and one 8-bit value of Cr are assigned. The result is an average of 12 bits per pixel.

Z

Z: See Z-Axis.

Z Value: The value that represents distance from the eye point in a Z-buffer rendering system.

Z-Axis: A term that measures the depth of an object in a 3D world. Each object is composed of a group of vertices (points) that form polygons, which in turn combine to form a complex object.

Z-Buffer: An additional portion of memory that stores a 3D object's value on the Z-axis (depth). Z-buffering tracks the depth of each triangle's vertices from the viewer's perspective, and sorts the triangles to ensure that only front objects are drawn.

ZIP: A compressed file format (.zip). Many files available on the Internet are compressed, or zipped, in order to reduce storage space and transfer times.

Zoetrope: An early animation device that uses strips of sequential drawings that are spun and viewed through slits in a rotating drum to create an illusion of motion.

Zoom: Only the camera's simulated focal length is modified, while its position and orientation remain untouched.

Zoom Tool: A tool used to magnify the current image.

Z-Sorting: The process of removing hidden surfaces by sorting polygons in a back-to-front order prior to rendering; less accurate than Z-buffering.

Contributing Organizations and Companies

Half-Life; The New School; Internet Movie Database, Today's Video; Adobe Systems; Epic Multimedia; KCTS; Eastman Kodak; Annenberg/CPB; Quantel, Inc; FilmSecrets; Special Interest Video Sales Group; TV Cameraman; Video Demystified; Videofonics; Zerocut; University of Maryland; DVD Made Easy; CyberCollege; Encoda Systems; Video Essentials. EZ DVD Advisor; iLearn; Compression Works; TV Guide; Sweetwater; Television: Critical Methods and Applications, University of Alabama; Calvert; Net Composite; Grantastic Designs; Third Millennium Entertainment; SVN, Inc.; Silcone Valley North, Inc.; Motto; Virtual Worlds; Apple; Cleaver Brooks; EKEDA; Prolink USA; System 16 Arcade Museum; Webopedia; California Department of Education; Eye on Video; Tippett Studio; Florida Department of Education; Internet Campus; Planet Quake; Intellisoft; Australian Centre for the Moving Image; Sympatico; The Scratch Post; Introduction to Film, Berkeley; Arts Act; Animation USA; Demon Internet; Utah State University; DUMC Department of Surgery Digital Media Guide; Kitezh; Bergen; Profim, S.A.; Meisler; Aigcorp; Hewlett Packard; Digital Exposure; Digital Director; Mississippi State University; 4-K Associates; Cobalt Systems; Gallery Direct; Chem Co.; The Way Computer Graphics Works; SalmonIdaho; Digital TV Zone; Design In You; High End 3D; Canon; Rendering with Radiance; 3D Technology; CyberEdge; SoftImage Effect Web; ACM SIGGRAPH; DVD Made Easy; Nonoctave; Source Forge; University of Toronto; Audio Education; Video Guys; Products, Services, and Ideas.com; Realsoft; IT-Director; Alias/Wavefront; IPSI Imaging; The Ohio State University; Wallstreet Webs; Computer Science Society; Survey of Medical VR; Soft Landmark; OpenGL Performer Getting Started Guide; Ripon Printers; Future Technology; University of Maryland, Baltimore County; Unicom Telecommunication; DIT Imaging; Guru 3D; Bib2Web; PLASMA; Crossbow Technology; JPG Digital; The APECS Performance Animation System; Directron; International Hydrocut; Domain Decomposition of Geometrical Objects; Vintage Ink & Paint; Media Value; Internet Campus; Alaska Fisheries Information Network; University of California Los Angeles; Botics Computer Consulting.

Bibliography
Selected Books

Adobe Systems, Inc. Adobe Photoshop 5.5: Classroom in a Book. Adobe Press. 1999.

Culhane, Shamus. Animation from Script to Screen. St. Martin's Press, New York. 1988.

Finch, Christopher. Special Effects: Creating Movie Magic. Cross River Press. New York 1984.

Fry, Ron, and Pamela Rourzon. The Saga of Special Effects. Prentice-Hall International, New Jersey. 1977.

Gardner, Garth. Informal Computer-Art Education. Unpublished Dissertation. Ohio State University. 1995.

Gardner, Garth. Careers in Computer Graphics and Animation. GGC Publishing. Washington, DC. 2000.

Gardner, Garth. Computer Graphics and Animation: History, Careers, Expert Advice. GGC Publishing, Washington, DC. 2002

Kerlow, Isaac Victor. The Art Of 3-D Computer Animation and Imaging, John Wiley & Sons, Inc. New York. 2002.

Kerlow, Isaac Victor, and Judson Rosebush. Computer Graphics for Designers and Artists. Van Nostrand Reinhold. New York. 1986.

Laybourne, Kit. The Animation Book. Crown Traders Paperbacks, New York. 1979.

Lopuck, Lisa. Designing Multimedia. Peachpit Press, Berkeley, CA. 1996.

Lord, Peter, and Brian Sibley. Creating 3-D Animation: The Aardman Book of Filmmaking. Harry N. Abrams, Inc. New York. 1998.

Masson, Terrence. CG 101: A Computer Graphic Industry Reference. New Riders Publishing, Indianapolis. 1999.

Morrison, Mike. Becoming A Computer Animator. Sams Publishing, Indianapolis. 1994.

Olson, Robert. Art Direction For Film and Video. Focal Press, Boston London. 1993.

Roberts, Jason, and Phil Gross. Director Demystified 7. Macromedia Press, Peachpit Press, Berkeley, CA. 1999.

Webber, Marilyn. Gardner's Guide to Animation Scriptwriting: The Writer's Road Map. GGC Publishing, Washington D.C. 2000.

Webber, Marilyn. Gardner's Guide to Feature Animation Screenwriting: The Writer's Road Map. GGC Publishing, Washington D.C. 2002.

Zettl, Herbert. Television Production Handbook, 6th Edition. Wadsworth Publishing Company. Belmont, CA. 1997.

GARTH GARDNER COMPANY

GGC publishing

Washington DC, USA · London, UK

Other GARDNER'S Guides

Gardner's Guide to Careers in Computer Graphics & Animation

Gardner's Guide to Computer Graphics and Animation: History, Careers, Expert Advice

Gardner's Guide to Television Scriptwriting: The Writer's Road Map

Gardner's Guide to Animation Scriptwriting: The Writer's Road Map

Gardner's Guide to Screenwriting: The Writer's Road Map

Gardner's Guide to Feature Animation Writing: The Writer's Road Map

Gardner's Guide to Colleges for Multimedia & Animation

Gardner's Storyboard Sketchbook

Gardner's Guide to Multimedia and Animation Studios

Gardner's Guide to internships in New Media

orders@ggcinc.com
www.gogardner.com